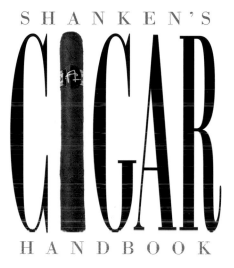

SHANKEN'S

CIGAR

HANDBOOK

CIGAR
Aficionado

SHANKEN'S
CIGAR
HANDBOOK

A Connoisseur's Guide to Smoking Pleasure

By Marvin R. Shanken,

publisher of *Cigar Aficionado*

and *Marvin Shanken's Cigar Insider* newsletter

Foreword by Bill Cosby

RUNNING PRESS
PHILADELPHIA · LONDON

M. SHANKEN COMMUNICATIONS, INC.
NEW YORK

9   8   7   6   5   4   3   2   1

Digit on the right indicates the number of this printing

Library of Congress Cataloging-in-Publication Number 96-71937

ISBN 0-7624-0086-2

For subscriptions to *Cigar Aficionado*, please call: (800) 992-2442
Or write:
M. Shanken Communications
387 Park Avenue South
New York, New York 10016

Visit our website at:
http://www.cigaraficionado.com

This book may be ordered by mail from the publisher.
Please include $2.50 for postage and handling.
But try your bookstore first!

Running Press Book Publishers
125 South Twenty-second Street
Philadelphia, Pennsylvania 19103-4399

To my wife, Hazel, my father, Oscar,
and in loving memory of my mother, Evelyn.

ACKNOWLEDGEMENTS

I would like to thank the following people who contributed
to the making of this book: At M. Shanken Communications, Inc.,
Michael Moaba, Gordon Mott, George Brightman, Ann Berkhausen,
David Savona, Amy Lyons, Martin Leeds, and Shawn Vale.
At Running Press, Stuart "Buz" Teacher, David Borgenicht,
Greg Jones, and Ken Newbaker.

TABLE OF CONTENTS

FOREWORD 8

INTRODUCTION 11

CHAPTER 1 THE CIGAR SMOKING EXPERIENCE
One of Life's Great Pleasures 24

CHAPTER 2 SELECTING PREMIUM CIGARS
The Choice is Yours 32

CHAPTER 3 MARVIN R. SHANKEN'S
TOP 40 CIGAR BRANDS 40

CHAPTER 4 PREPARING TO SMOKE:
CUTTING AND LIGHTING YOUR CIGAR
The Tricks of the Trade 82

CHAPTER 5 ETIQUETTE TIPS
The Keys to Cultured Smoking 90

CHAPTER 6 STORING CIGARS
Protect Your Collection 96

CHAPTER 7 THE GEOGRAPHY OF
CIGAR TOBACCO CULTIVATION
From Cuba to Connecticut 108

CHAPTER 8 THE MAKING OF PREMIUM CIGARS
The Art of the Torcedor 116

CHAPTER 9 CIGAR COLORS, SHAPES, AND SIZES
There's Something for Everyone 122

CHAPTER 10 CIGARS AND SPIRITS
A Fruitful Marriage 132

CHAPTER 11 A CENTURY OF CIGARS
From King Edward VII to Cigar Aficionado *Magazine* . . . 146

APPENDIX CIGAR BRAND DIRECTORY 166

GLOSSARY 197

INDEX 205

FOREWORD

by Bill Cosby

When I light up a good cigar, I describe it by saying: "This is a good cigar." But merely saying a cigar is good isn't good enough anymore. Describing a cigar's flavor these days requires a palate so discerning that it can recognize such things as "herbal earthiness with coffee bean and cinnamon tones, leather notes, and a woody finish." To see what that means, I suppose I could take a sprig of parsley, a handful of dirt, some coffee beans, a dash of cinnamon, an old shoe, and a piece of wood, then roll it all into a Connecticut Shade wrapper and smoke it. On the other hand, I think I'll just stick with the contents of my humidor and simply say that my cigars taste like tobacco.

During the last couple of years, as cigars grew in popularity, somebody decided that all these new cigar chompers needed a social destination where they could smoke without being yelled at by other customers. Hence, the cigar bar. However, while every cigar may have its own pleasant aroma, when you take 200 people smoking 90 brands and put them in one room, you wind up with a cloud of smog more deadly than the atmosphere of Los Angeles on a bad day. Once, when I wandered into one of these wood-paneled little rooms, I detected the bouquet of a foot in need of Lubriderm. It turned out not to be a foot at all; rather it was a robusto clenched between someone's teeth. I also identified such scents as rotting leaves from an October lawn, old FedEx stuffings, fresh dog droppings, rubber with tones of earwax, plastic with a hint of nylon, an old telephone from the 1930s, damp newspapers, and fillers made of discarded vacuum cleaner bags. I haven't smelled a burning sock yet, but then again, a new cigar bar opens every day.

My advice to those of you on your way to a cigar bar is this: *Never* take your best cigars. Take your third or fourth best cigars. Or better yet, find a small stick, drill a hole through the center, and smoke that. With all the other foul fogs wafting into your nose, you won't be able to tell the difference between a stick and a Hoyo anyway.

All tobacco leaves are made by God and therefore all tobacco leaves are wonderful. Only man can take a perfectly wonderful leaf and turn it into a bad cigar. Or—God forgive me—into a cigarette! I can't speak for God but I would dare say that when God made tobacco He envisioned hand-rolled double coronas and not machine-made Ultra Light 100s.

For a cigar smoker, a cigar is a more than enough sensory stimulation all by itself. But a cigarette smoker, extracting no taste from the nicotine haze he inhales into his lungs, will resort to chewing gum while he smokes. (Imagine drawing on a Cohiba with a Chiclet in your mouth!) I have even seen cigarette smokers puff away during a meal.

Besides never eating while I smoke, there is one food I can't eat before I smoke. Nuts. When I do happen to have a handful of nuts, I rinse out my mouth prior to lighting up a cigar. Otherwise, when a little piece of nut dislodges from my teeth, I can't be sure if it's a remnant of cashew or a fragment of tobacco from the end of my cigar. And swallowing tobacco disturbs my peristalysis.

I'm not telling *you* what you should or shouldn't do, I'm just relating what *I* can't do. In the end, you see, it all comes down to personal taste. If you're a cigar aficionado and you want to describe your corona as having "a hint of mint with piano notes and a fried filet finish," go right ahead.

As for me, I'm going to sit down and pull out a little treat I've been saving for some time. It has hints of toasted oats and dried fruit with cinnamon notes and a cocoa finish. No, it's not a cigar.

It's a chocolate granola bar.

INTRODUCTION

Marvin R. Shanken

I t's important to me that my cigar book communicate to you not just the basic facts about cigars, but also some of the passion many of us feel for cigars, and a sense of how far cigar appreciation has come in the United States in just a few short years. To do that, I want you to know what I had to go through to learn about cigars, what was involved in launching *Cigar Aficionado* magazine, and some of the challenges I expect us to face in the coming years.

How I Learned About Fine Cigars

If you are just beginning to learn the joys of premium handmade cigars, you may not realize how lonely it was to be a cigar aficionado in the United States, and how hard it was to find out about fine cigars, as recently as just a few years ago— particularly for someone whose family had no real tradition of

Cigar Aficionado *celebrated its 1992 launch with a gala party at the* St. Regis Hotel *rooftop ballroom in New York City.*

connoisseurship. Ironically, although I am the publisher of *Wine Spectator* and *Cigar Aficionado* magazines, I come from a family that didn't drink at all, and never, ever smoked cigars.

I myself had no interest in beer, wine, liquor, cigarettes, or cigars during high school. However, in college, I began to smoke inexpensive cigars: Hav-a-tampa Jewels, which, as I recall, were five for a quarter and came with wooden tips. I'm not sure whether I smoked them because I liked the taste, or because I liked the feeling of sophistication they gave me as a nineteen-year-old.

After college, I started working on Wall Street for a small investment banking firm, and it was there that I first gained an inkling of the idea of cigar smoking as a part of a better lifestyle. In my mid-twenties, I began smoking Royal Jamaica cigars, which I found to be mild and very enjoyable, as well as a number of other lesser known brands. I thought it was a big deal that I had a humidor, but, in fact, I knew very little about cigar appreciation, and frankly knew of nowhere to turn to learn more.

Smoking cigars in the seventies and eighties was very unpopular and frowned upon in the United States. I would look forward to vacations in the Caribbean and business trips to Europe, particularly London, where I felt free to light up and where I could discover more about the cigar lifestyle.

I have vivid memories of going to London on business in the late seventies and early eighties. When I arrived at the airport, I would have the driver take me directly to the Davidoff store on the corner of St. James and Jermyn Streets so I could hand pick my stock of Cuban cigars to smoke while I was over there. If the store was closed because I was too early or too late,

Baroness Philippine de Rothschild, proprietor of the famed Bordeaux Château Mouton-Rothschild, was given the first Cigar Aficionado *Man of the Year award at the launch party. The legendary Zino Davidoff sat with her.*

I was very, very disappointed. Visiting the local cigar shops was the highlight of my European trips, even more than dining at three-star restaurants.

I never went to London without making the circuit of the great cigar shops there, particularly Robert Lewis, Davidoff (of course), Alfred Dunhill, Desmond Sauter, and J.J. Fox. The proprietors and the clerks who worked in these stores seemed bemused by this American who had a huge enthusiasm for cigars and wanted to learn as much as he could. Their attitude, for the most part, was "what's the big deal?" They had been selling cigars, and, in particular, Cuban cigars, for a hundred years or more. But, to an American, the experience of being in a country where Cuban cigars are readily available (spell that legal) and appreciated was an extraordinary treat.

Why and How *Cigar Aficionado* Magazine Was Launched

My involvement with cigars has always been more of a personal passion than a business venture. My reason for telling the story of *Cigar Aficionado* is not to brag—as you will see, luck played a big role in its success, and many of my decisions were, well . . . illogical. I want you to know the saga of the magazine because it is powerful inspiration for budding aficionados; it is proof that there are many out there who are proud of the pleasure they take from smoking handmade cigars.

I wrote the phrase "cigar aficionado" for the first time in my column "I Love a Good Smoke . . ." in the February, 1984, issue of *Wine Spectator*, almost a decade before I launched the cigar magazine with that name. I was writing about an historic auction that was held in December, 1983, at the 7th Regiment Armory at Park Avenue and 67th Street in New York City. The auction had been organized by J.R. Tobacco's legendary (even then) Lew Rothman. For the first time since Cuban products were embargoed in 1962, Cuban cigars were legally up for bid; all the cigars in the auction had been made before the embargo. The major networks covered the event, and publicity-hungry buyers bid the first 15 or 20 lots to prices well in excess of their realistic value. I waited out the initial frenzy and acquired a good-sized lot of small pre-Castro Flor de Farachs at a reasonable price.

It's appropriate that the name "Cigar Aficionado" should have appeared first in *Wine Spectator* since the success of that publication was integral to the later launching of *Cigar Aficionado*. First of all, as editor and publisher of *Wine Spectator*, I had developed an editorial

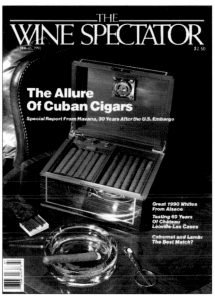

The success of this issue of Wine Spectator *(2/15/92) played an integral part in the launch of* Cigar Aficionado.

formula for publishing a magazine I had a passion for. More to the point, I was willing to use funds generated by *Wine Spectator* to subsidize a potentially unprofitable cigar magazine, if I had to.

In 1991, I challenged the editors of *Wine Spectator* to come up with new ideas to expand the editorial content far beyond wine. I had in mind topics such as travel, dining, cooking and collecting. One of the editors suggested cigars. At first, I rejected the idea because years ago, after I had done the *Spectator* column on cigars, I had received a lot of needling from my senior editors who thought it improper, incorrect and insensitive, to say the least, to put an article on cigars in a wine magazine. (I, of course, was a strong supporter of more articles on cigars in *Wine Spectator*, but had backed off in response to the criticism from the editors, none of whom were cigar lovers at that time.)

The editors, however, pressed the idea of a feature on

Cuban cigars by pounding the table and chanting "cov-er, cov-er." When I asked who should write it, they pointed to me. So, in the fall of 1991, I went to Cuba with James Suckling, our London-based European Bureau Chief. He and I spent a week there researching the cover story of the February, 1992, issue of *Wine Spectator*, entitled "The Allure of Cuban Cigars."

It was one of the most exciting weeks of my life. I felt like a child left alone in F.A.O. Schwartz, or a woman at Tiffany's or Cartier with an unlimited budget. The excitement was heightened by the fact that the trip seemed a little risky: just before my departure a professional Cuba-watcher warned me not to go because of a possible coup.

As it turned out, we were never in danger; in fact, we were warmly welcomed everywhere from the fields and sheds in the Vuelta Abajo, the premium tobacco and wrapper-growing area for Cuban cigars, to the factories in Havana. The high point was our tour of the legendary Romeo y Julieta factory, which has been making cigars since 1914. The cigar rollers, who had been told that we were American journalists, began banging their *chavetas*, or cutting knives, on their work benches. When it was explained to us that this was their traditional form of applause and welcome, I got goose bumps. I remained moved by this for many weeks afterwards.

I was so inspired by the whole experience that while I was returning home, I looked out the airplane window and said to myself "I'm 48 years old; you only go around once. The hell with it! I'm gonna do a cigar magazine!"

I knew I would need this kind of raw dedication to succeed. Cigar consumption in the U.S. had declined from around 9 billion cigars in the early 1960's to 2 billion in the early '90's. In addition, the allegations about second-hand smoke were becoming widely accepted, and more and more establishments, both public and private, were restricting or eliminating cigar smoking. Also, many people just didn't like the smell of cigars. To say that cigar smoking was out of favor was a huge understatement.

On top of that, the publishing industry in the early 1990's had just gone through several years of softness. Many publications had closed down, and a number of publishing houses had resorted to layoffs in order to keep their overhead under control—M. Shanken Communications, Inc. included.

Nonetheless, without any research, business plan, or budget, I went back to New York and called a meeting of my publishing team. There were about eight of us in the conference room when I announced that I was going to launch a cigar publication. I looked around the room, and there was not one smile. All of my key managerial team were shocked. Everyone said I should go very, very slowly. In fact, one of my staff suggested that I publish a single issue as an insert to *Wine Spectator* and forget the idea of doing a cigar magazine, for which there was clearly no market. But I was committed to doing a cigar magazine, and frankly, nothing would stop me.

When I related my plans to some of the people in the cigar trade, they encouraged me, in the hopes that a publication might help their ailing businesses. But the inside joke in the industry was "make sure you get the first issue, because it's going to become a collector's item." Nobody thought a second issue would ever get published.

Cigar rollers at the Romeo y Julieta factory in Havana, Cuba.

My friends in the advertising and publishing communities were just as negative. I remember vividly that several of my friends repeated the same phrase: "Marvin, you've lost your mind." They predicted that not only would I lose a great deal of money, I would also hurt my reputation as a publisher. Even the reaction from the businessmen in my YPO (Young Presidents Organization) forum, almost all of whom smoked cigars, was negative. Some of them were adamantly opposed, but a few said "what the hell, why not try it?" The more my friends joked about my dream—Marvin's folly—the more determined I became to prove them wrong.

Even I underestimated the size of the audience which would be interested in a cigar magazine. I was hoping that there would be 15,000 to 20,000 cigar nuts like me out there, and I fully expected to lose a significant sum of money each year for the rest of my life to publish it.

The marketing campaign used to launch *Cigar Aficionado* was among the most amateurish you could imagine. It consisted of a 1/6-page black and white ad which read: "Wanted: Cigar lovers. I don't have a name, I don't have a date, I don't have a price, and I don't have a frequency, but I plan on coming out with a cigar magazine and if you want to get the first issue with my complements please write or fax me and we'll put you on the list." The only place I ran the ad was in *Wine Spectator.*

This was a stroke of pure luck. I later discovered what in hindsight seems obvious: the same people who smoked, drank, and the same people who drank, smoked. The demographics and psychographics of cigar smokers and fine wine drinkers/collectors were nearly identical. *Wine Spectator*'s male-dominated subscriber list was perfect for promoting the launch of a cigar magazine.

At first, I would get one or two responses a day; then after a few weeks I would get five or ten a day, and, after a while, 40 or 50 a day. I also supplied cigar retailers with postcards to give out to their customers, and this generated even more names and addresses. By the time I launched the magazine, as a quarterly, I had roughly 25,000–30,000 requests for the first issue.

Most magazines need both readers and advertisers to survive. My projections of the number of advertisers who would be interested in *Cigar Aficionado* were as pessimistic as my estimate of readership. There were very few handmade cigar brands that advertised in the U.S. in 1991, and their business volume was low. I knew of six. Macanudo had the largest share, followed by four or five other brands including Te-Amo, H. Upmann, Partagas, Davidoff, and Dunhill, and that was basically it. I also thought that I had a fair chance of getting some of the distilled spirits companies to advertise because of the very clear association of Cognac, Scotch, and Port with cigars. In addition, I was hoping that some luxury advertisers would be interested, but I thought that was a limited market because of the potential of being stigmatized for being associated with a cigar or tobacco publication.

Cigar Aficionado exceeded these expectations, too, in part because of the efforts of its editorial and business team which consisted of Gordon Mott, George Brightman, and James Suckling. Mott had been the managing editor for another of my publications, *Market Watch*, but had written a freelance article several years earlier on cigars for *The New York Times*. He became CA's managing editor. Brightman had spent 15 years in the tobacco business, most recently as the manager of the Davidoff store on Madison Avenue in New York, and before that a decade at Georgetown Tobacco in Washington. He had an encyclopedic knowledge of cigars and the cigar trade. Suckling, who was with me on my original fact-finding trip to Cuba in 1991, was then and is still European Bureau Chief of *Wine Spectator* in addition to his duties at *Cigar Aficionado*. He and I had many, many talks about what CA should and should not be. CA would not be, could not be, all that it became without Gordon, George, and Jim.

With this group, I developed the concept for *Cigar Aficionado*. We decided to make it a glossy magazine with stories on cigars and cigar regions, with tastings and ratings similar to *Spectator*'s, plus profiles of famous personalities and historical information.

I saw the magazine as not just a cigar lover's magazine, but really as a men's lifestyle magazine. I wanted it to cover the whole gamut of things that men did for pleasure, whether it was vactioning, drinking, gambling, golf, collecting, you name it. Whatever it was, we wanted to do it with great style.

I refused to get discouraged when potential readers and advertisers would say to me, "Why should we read a cigar magazine when it comes to collecting? There are half a dozen art and antiques magazines out there." Or, "Why should I be interested in what you have to say about travel when there are a number of travel magazines available?" Or, "Why should I be interested in what you have to say about golf?" I told them that ours was going to be a different approach, but many of them didn't understand the concept until we actually started publishing the magazine.

One of the decisions I made in developing the magazine was to entitle the letters section "Dear Marvin," as opposed to "To The Editor." I felt that I had such strong personal convictions regarding cigars that I wanted to make a personal statement, no matter how popular or unpopular it might be. I knew that by connecting myself personally with cigar smoking, I was taking a position that would be controversial, if not dangerous, especially if the magazine failed, but was driven to do so by my commitment and belief in what I was doing.

The launch of the magazine in September, 1992, was celebrated with a black-tie dinner on the rooftop of the St. Regis hotel in New York City, with approximately 200 cigar lovers and members of the cigar trade from all over the world in attendance. We gave our first "Man of the Year" award to Mme. Philippine de Rothschild of Château Mouton-Rothschild, who had also been a long-time cigar smoker. The long list of other luminaries who spoke at this occasion includes Edgar M. Cullman, Zino Davidoff and Nick Freeman from London,

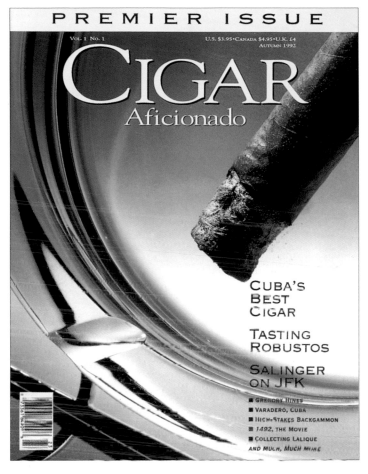

PREMIER ISSUE

VOL. 1 No. 1   U.S. $3.95•CANADA $4.95•U.K. £4
AUTUMN 1992

CIGAR
Aficionado

CUBA'S
BEST
CIGAR

TASTING
ROBUSTOS

SALINGER
ON JFK

■ GREGORY HINES
■ VARADERO, CUBA
■ HIGH-STAKES BACKGAMMON
■ 1492, THE MOVIE
■ COLLECTING LALIQUE
AND MUCH, MUCH MORE

David Tang from Hong Kong, Lew Rothman from J. R. Tobacco, Danny Blumenthal from Villazon, Phil Guarascio of General Motors, entertainer Gregory Hines, Oscar Boruchin from Miami, and many more.

The rest, as they say, is history. The first four years of *Cigar Aficionado* magazine exceeded all of our wildest dreams. We have carried ads from all segments of the economy. The growth in paid circulation, which as I write this is more than 400,000 (total readership exceeds a million), has been even more astonishing. Every issue has brought a dramatic increase in the size of the print run. The magazine is truly an international success with readers in nearly 100 countries around the world.

My readers wrote me that they loved *Cigar Aficionado*, but because it was a quarterly magazine, they had to wait three months for every new issue. So in December 1996 we launched a monthly newsletter, *Marvin Shanken's Cigar Insider*, which provides extensive and timely cigar information and cigar ratings. And in 1997 *Cigar Aficionado* became bimonthly, publishing six issues per year.

In 1997 we were honored to receive the "Acres of Diamonds" award from Temple University's School of Communication and Theater for best consumer magazine launched in the past five years. Previous winners include *Smart Money*, *Sports Illustrated For Kids*, and *Martha Stewart Living*—not bad company!

The Future We Face

For cigar smokers, the atmosphere is a lot more pleasant in the United States today than it was just a few years ago. In the very first issue which listed cigar-friendly restaurants, we were able, after great research, to come up with only about 50 establishments. Today, of course, the list includes thousands of cigar-friendly restaurants and hotels across America. We had a section which listed cigar events—smoker dinners and so forth—and there were fewer than twenty once-a-year affairs. Today there are too many events to count!

I am often asked to explain the strength of the cigar movement. I believe that there are numerous factors that have led men—and recently, women—to cigars, but that most of all, it comes down to people wanting to have fun with their lives and do things that they enjoy. Cigars not only are fun, they taste great, they're sophisticated, and smoking them is a wonderful form of relaxation.

There are other popular explanations. Some people say it's backlash against the "in your face" attitude of anti-smokers. Others point to the romance of Cuba. Still others attribute it to the aura of power, success, and sophistication that accompanies the image of a person smoking a cigar. The reasons are countless.

But I feel it would be a great mistake to just assume that we will always be free to practice our pleasure. Due in part to the tremendous media attention that cigars have attracted in recent years, cigar smoking has drawn intense fire from the health police—most notably the American Cancer Society. They've been trying to discourage cigarette smoking for a long time, and now they're going after cigars—despite the fact that, at this time, there is very little clear research on cigars alone. They are using cigarette research data and extrapolating the implications to cigar smokers without the definitive documentation necessary to substantiate their claims. I don't expect this situation to change in the foreseeable future.

My hope is that one day there will be research which clearly shows the risks of cigar smoking. As cigar smokers know, we do not inhale. Moreover cigars, unlike cigarettes, are not addictive. In my conversations with many doctors who are themselves cigar smokers (and subscribers to the magazine), I have heard that if you smoke cigars moderately—CA readers average one cigar a day or less—the risks are small or limited, and not at all analogous to the risks incurred by cigarette chain-smokers who may inhale the smoke from as many as one to three packs a day.

Whether cigar smoking is worth the possible health risks and probable rudeness of some rabid anti-smokers is, ultimately, a personal issue that each smoker must face. But it's not an issue you should have to face alone. As long as I have anything to do with it, there will be a reputable magazine which will give you the facts and information relevant to your chosen lifestyle and pursuit of happiness.

As always, light up with a smile.

Marvin R. Shanken
April 1997

CHAPTER I
THE CIGAR SMOKING EXPERIENCE
One of Life's Great Pleasures

Cigars provide a unique smoking experience. To start with, only certain genetic strains of tobacco are used in cigars, and the tobacco is generally raised and aged with exquisite care. Cigar tobacco loses a lot of its nicotine during the fermentation process.

Cigars are designed to burn at unusually low temperatures. This means that the tobacco doesn't carbonize or overheat, so the flavor stays mellow. In addition to its superior flavor, the simple fact that cigar smoke is cool helps make cigars a most pleasant smoke.

Like food and wine, smoke is experienced by the taste receptors on the tongue, and to some extent on the roof of the mouth. The four basic taste components are sweet, sour, salty, and bitter. But, as with food and wine, cigar smoke can deliver an endless variety of flavors. Not surprisingly, the vocabulary used to describe cigars echoes the vocabulary used for gourmet cuisine, fine wines, and spirits: words like acidic, salty, bitter, sweet, harsh, sour, smooth, heavy, full-bodied, rich, and balanced. There are also those who expand their cigar vocabulary to include more pretentious terms such as mellifluous, transcendent, and opaque.

A cigar can contain several different flavors. Each flavor can have a different body and intensity. Each puff can have a different initial taste and aftertaste. And each cigar can change as it is smoked. Also, there are variations you can create by smoking a cigar while eating different foods or drinking different spirits.

But that's just the mouth's experience. Cigars are also

enjoyed by the nose, the hand, and the eye. The pleasures of cigar smoking are varied enough to keep a smoker enchanted for a lifetime!

Many cultured people are learning that the art of smoking a cigar is an elegant, leisurely activity. Done correctly, it will help you slow down and relax, no matter how hectic your life is.

The measured breathing of a cigar aficionado has been compared to the steady breathing of an experienced meditator. Like effective meditation, cigar smoking energizes you. Cigars can act as stimulants. You will find that they give you a pleasant lift— they sharpen your senses and increase your sense of well-being.

The Art of Cigar Smoking

Bring the lit cigar to your lips and blow the first puff out to expel any harsh flavors left over from lighting, then take your first inward puff. Let the cool smoke swirl into your mouth, but don't inhale. Remove the cigar from your mouth. Savor the flavors and gently exhale. Wait a moment before you take your next puff.

Chewing on a cigar, or holding the cigar between your teeth while your hands are otherwise occupied, is not a good idea. You're likely to end up with a wet, compressed stub that doesn't draw well. It's not pleasant or pretty.

Don't be reluctant to put your cigar down in an ashtray for a few seconds now and then. As long as you take a puff every minute, a well-made cigar should stay lit.

Smile. You are enjoying one of life's great pleasures!

When you are through, don't "stub out" your cigar. Extinguishing it as you would a cigarette will release unpleasant odors from the remaining tars. Simply place your cigar in an ashtray—it will go out by itself, without producing extra smoke. Dispose of butts quickly to avoid lingering aromas.

How to Hold Your Cigar

Hold a cigar like a lover: gently, but firmly. Do not squeeze it between two fingers as if it were a cigarette—you're likely to damage it or to restrict the free flow of smoke. Aficionados are most comfortable and get the best control using a thumb and one or two opposing fingers.

As you gain experience, you will find that your hands tell you a lot about a cigar, even before you cut and light it. In fact, an important test of how well a cigar has been manufactured and maintained is how it feels when held.

Before you know it, you'll become familiar with the feel of a cigar that has been properly hand-rolled and humidified. It is firm, but slightly elastic; it gives a little when you apply gentle pressure with your fingertips. It does not feel, or sound, dry. It has no soft spots which could lead to harsh-flavored fast burning and no hard spots which could limit the cigar's "draw" and make it go out between puffs. You will develop "finger-memory" of what a properly humidified cigar feels like.

Tom Selleck enjoys a smoke at "A Night to Remember" charity dinner in April 1997.

As time goes on, you may even learn to distinguish silky-smooth Connecticut Shade wrapper leaves from wrappers with more texture, or tooth, with your eyes closed. The only way to acquire this level of skill is through experience, so be sure to focus on the characteristics of each cigar you pick up.

Smoking Outdoors

Smoking a cigar in the open air is one of life's great pleasures. There are few experiences more exhilarating than smoking while looking at clouds or the stars. Given social pressures, outdoors is sometimes the only place one can comfortably smoke.

Some purists claim you should never smoke while doing anything else—you should concentrate on your cigar experience. In our opinion, however, there is nothing wrong with smoking while strolling or while traversing the golf course. Smoking while running, or doing anything else that prohibits slow, relaxed breathing is, however, self-defeating.

Try to smoke in an area that's relatively sheltered from strong winds so the breeze doesn't accelerate your cigar's combustion. Shorter cigars are generally easier to shelter and thus are better

President Clinton often enjoys chomping on a fine cigar while relaxing on the golf course.

in windy conditions. And keep in mind that a strong breeze will dilute the cigar's aroma, and perhaps prevent ash formation.

If you smoke outdoors with any frequency, you'll want to carry a lighter (gas, not fluid). Getting a good, even light from matches in a breeze is challenging for even the most adept smoker.

If you are planning on smoking outside during the day, be sure your fingers aren't coated with sunblock. Cigars absorb chemicals quickly, and if you read the ingredients on a tube of sunblock you'll know they're not something you want to smoke.

If you are smoking in a dry area, don't discard used matches or cigar stubs: carry them out with you. Don't, however, worry about discarding the end cut from a cigar or cool ashes: cigars are one of the most natural, organic products imaginable.

Choosing a Cigar to Fit Your Face

The cigar that best fits your face is the cigar that gives you the most contented smile. Beyond that, don't worry. Brandy connoisseurs with round faces don't avoid snifters.

Watching Your Ash

Experienced connoisseurs can rate other people's cigars from across a room. They have two important indicators to go by: the aroma factor and the ash. The aroma is obvious: a high-quality cigar just smells better than a bad one. Ash is a little more subtle. Its color is important. Generally, the whiter the ash, the finer the soil in which the tobacco was grown. The structure of the ash counts, too. A fine cigar will grow a sizable ash tip, which often reflects the tight construction of the cigar.

At some cigar dinners, there are contests to see who can grow the longest ash. This can be an amusing diversion on occasion, but generally you'll want to flick off your ash before it drops on you, the furniture, or the carpet. Long-time smokers like to claim that cigar ashes are actually good for carpets—they supposedly absorb and bind oils which can damage the fabric. This may be true, but most hosts and hostesses are unaware of it, and they tend to look askance at ash droppers. It's better to put ashes in an ashtray.

CHAPTER 2
SELECTING PREMIUM CIGARS
The Choice Is Yours

Most of us approach our first few cigar purchases with a sweaty-palmed nervousness similar to other "first-time" experiences. It's a complicated process: we're not completely sure we know what we are doing, and the chances of making an embarrassing gaffe are pretty good.

It doesn't have to be that way. Good tobacconists, like good wine merchants, are almost always ready to spend time educating beginners. Besides, there really is no way to make a mistake when choosing cigars. It's a matter of personal taste—whatever you like is what is right.

One way to become more comfortable with buying cigars is to spend some time in a fine tobacco shop. Keep your eyes, ears, and nostrils open. Listen to the conversation and ask a few questions. Learn a bit about the difference between Connecticut Shade and Cuban Seed cigar wrappers. Get to know the silky touch of perfectly-humidified cigars that are exuding a bit of oil. Feel the tooth texture of a Cameroon wrapper. Smell the difference between spicy cigars and milder ones as your fellow customers light up. What's more, when in a store, you can always fall back on the trick that experienced diners use in countries where they can't read the menu: point to something someone else is savoring and say, "I'll have one of those."

In no time, you will develop your own point of view. You'll find yourself having opinions, and the experience to back them up. You'll know what a maduro wrapper looks like. You'll know the dimensional difference between a pyramid and a torpedo. You'll have a sense of whether the manufacturer being discussed is improving its standards, or becoming less selective about the tobaccos it uses. You will notice that novices are leaning in to hear *your* words of wisdom.

Choosing a Tobacconist

Ideally, your tobacconist will become one of the most important professionals in your life—right up there with your lawyer, accountant, and tailor. Not only will you be spending a lot of time in his or her establishment, you will want to be among the first to hear about new products, new brands, and events such as cigar dinners. (This is no small privilege: in this era of limited cigar supply, it's often only the tobacconist's friends and loyal customers who have the opportunity to taste certain hard-to-get cigars.)

You may come to rely on your tobacconist to special-order cigars for you (and perhaps give you a break on large orders). Some tobacconists even keep privileged customers' stock in their humidified storage area.

Spending time in a tobacco shop and trying different cigars will help you develop your own personal tastes.

Alfred Dunhill Limited in London offers one of the world's finest selections of cigars and cigar accessories.

Even though your tobacconist may become one of your best friends, never hesitate to return a poorly constructed cigar for credit. You won't hurt his or her feelings. The tobacconist will, in turn, return the cigar to the distributor or manufacturer, who will generally be glad for the opportunity to replace the cigar, preserve a hard-won reputation, and keep a valued customer.

Since your tobacconist will be an important partner in your pursuit of fine cigars, you will want to choose him or her as carefully as you choose your cigars. One test is, quite simply, whether you like the establishment and the people. Is conversation easy? Do they seem to understand your tastes and preferences? Do you trust their recommendations—do they come up with suggestions that expand your cigar experience, or do they just seem to be pushing house brands? You are going to be buying a premium product at a premium price; it is reasonable to expect some degree of personalized service.

An equally important criterion when choosing a tobacconist is how well their cigars are stored. If you walk into a "Smoke Shop" and find that most of the space is devoted to detective magazines, horse-racing newspapers, and lottery machines, while the cigars are kept in a dusty glass display case next to yellowing easel cards filled with pen knives, pen lights, and dark glasses, you are probably not in a palace of fine cigar information. Ask about their cigars anyway—you might be pleasantly surprised. Some stores keep humidified stock hidden from view "in the back" and have a steady flow of customers who keep their stock rotating. If, however, you are presented with a cellophane-wrapped cigar from a box that says "Buy War Bonds" on the outside, feel free to decline.

Zino Davidoff (1906–1994) was one of the most influential and respected men in the cigar world.

On the other hand, if a store has a walk-in humidor, and the staff invites you to walk in and experience the soft, scented air bearing so much moisture that it feels much cooler than its temperature of 70 degrees—you may have found a paradise.

If there's any doubt in your mind about the quality of a tobacconist, buy a cigar. While you wouldn't want to maul a cigar you don't own, you can feel free to prod and pinch a cigar you've bought. Roll it between your fingers. If it feels soft, yet "so round, so firm, so fully packed," as an old cigarette ad used to say, the odds are it has been well cared for. If the wrapper makes crinkly noises, or it cracks or breaks, the cigar was not stored properly, and the tobacconist should never have sold it to you.

Once you've found a qualified tobacconist and formed a solid relationship, your main problem will be limiting your purchases to the number of cigars you can properly store. There is something deeply alluring and attractive about the gentlemanly (and gentlewomanly) ritual of selecting and acquiring cigars. As an exercise in personal taste and self-indulgence, it has few rivals.

Although buying cigars is a wonderful ritual, don't let the experience become ritualistic. Stay open to new cigar possibilities and to the fact that your tastes may change and mature. Certainly, you should always be well-stocked with your old favorites, but you should also experiment regularly in order to discover new favorites and expand your taste horizons.

Evaluating Cigars

Aficionados evaluate cigars and build a sense of what they like. Here are certain questions you should ask as you rate a cigar (note: when evaluating multiple cigars in one sitting, you should always begin with the milder ones and proceed to the stronger):

Flavor. Do *you* like how it tastes? What flavors, smells and sensations does it remind you of? Does it seem spicy or bland? How is the first taste of the cigar? What flavors linger in your mouth after you're done with the cigar, and how long do these flavors stay with you?

Don't worry about technical terms; use evocative comparisons like cocoa, coffee, vanilla, autumn leaves, and wet grass.

Appearance and Feel. How does the cigar feel to your hand and what does it look like? Does it feel moist, smooth, and

Choosing a tobacconist is a very important decision and should be done carefully. You may want to ask questions—and take notes.

consistently firm? Does the wrapper look consistent, or is it covered with blotches, spots, veins, or perhaps even nicks and tears? Does it, in short, look perfect—in proportion as well as in finish?

Gradually, you will develop a keen sensitivity to the colors and textures of a cigar.

Burn and Draw. Does it "smoke" easily—delivering cool, consistent, tasty smoke from the first puff to the last? Does it draw easily? Does it tend to go out? Does it burn quickly and fill your mouth with hot smoke?

The true test of a cigar's construction is in the smoking. If it "smokes" easily, it's well-made.

The Value of Variety

Different cigars are right for different occasions. If you have only fifteen minutes to spare between lunch and your next appointment, it would be a shame to light a cigar that might give you an hour's pleasure. On the other hand, if you are settling into a prolonged discussion about the meaning of life, the state of major league baseball, or whether the wedding should be formal or not, a sizable cigar is definitely appropriate.

Those who smoke several cigars a day usually smoke progressively stronger cigars. Others prefer only a light cigar before bed or count on a power smoke to wake up. Still others save stronger cigars for the weekend. Smoking is very personal. There are guidelines, but no rules.

Of course, if you want to be the perfect host as well as an aficionado, you will keep a selection of cigars which will please your friends' tastes as well as your own.

CHAPTER 3

MARVIN R. SHANKEN'S
TOP 40 CIGAR BRANDS

There are literally hundreds of cigar brands manufactured around the world today; some are sold
only in small regions, while others are available
worldwide. But there are certain brands that stand
out above all the others, and for a number of reasons. Some are
bestsellers. Others are generally known to deliver the most
consistently excellent flavors. And still others because they hold
a unique place in history.

There's a top 40 list for everything, and now here is my
Top 40 list of the most important cigar brands in the world, in
alphabetical order. There are spaces provided for you to record
pertinent information about each entry. Try them all! And enjoy!

TOP 40 CIGAR BRANDS INDEX

ARTURO FUENTE	42	HOYO DE MONTERREY & HOYO DE MONTERREY EXCALIBUR (HONDURAN)	62
ASHTON	43	JOYA DE NICARAGUA	63
ASHTRAL	44	LA AURORA	64
AVO	45	LA GLORIA CUBANA	65
BAUZA	46	LICENCIADOS	66
BERING	47	MACANUDO	67
BOLIVAR	48	MONTECRISTO (CUBAN)	68
COHIBA	49	MONTECRISTO (DOMINICAN)	69
CUESTA-REY	50	PADRON	70
DAVIDOFF	51	PARTAGAS (CUBAN)	71
DIAMOND CROWN	52	PARTAGAS (DOMINICAN)	72
DON DIEGO	53	PUNCH (CUBAN)	73
DON TOMAS	54	PUNCH (HONDURAN)	74
DUNHILL AGED CIGARS	55	RAMON ALLONES (CUBAN)	75
EL REY DEL MUNDO (HONDURAN)	56	ROMEO Y JULIETA (CUBAN)	76
FONSECA	57	ROMEO Y JULIETA (DOMINICAN)	77
FUENTE FUENTE OPUS X	58	ROYAL JAMAICA	78
H. UPMANN (CUBAN)	59	SIGNATURE COLLECTION BY SANTIAGO CABANA	79
H. UPMANN (DOMINICAN)	60	TE-AMO	80
HOYO DE MONTERREY (CUBAN)	61	ZINO	81

In the listings that follow, please note that if several countries are listed as the source of filler
for a certain brand, then each cigar's filler may be blended from two or more of them. However, when two or more countries are listed after binder or wrapper, it means that different
cigars in that brand use tobacco from different sources.

ARTURO FUENTE

Arturo Fuente is one of the best-selling cigar brands in the United States. It's also among the most difficult to find, even though Fuente shipped more than 13 million cigars in 1996. This company makes superbly crafted, flavorful smokes known for reasonable prices. Founded in Florida in 1912 by Arturo Fuente, the company had four factories damaged by fire in three countries before settling in the Dominican Republic. Today, the family heritage lives on in Carlos Fuente, Sr. and Carlos Fuente, Jr., who run what is now one of the largest handmade-cigar companies in the world. They recently opened a fourth factory in the Dominican Republic.

Manufactured in the Dominican Republic
Fillers/Binders: Dominican Republic
Wrappers: Cameroon

TASTING NOTES

CIGAR PURCHASED:

SIZE:

PLACE PURCHASED:

PURCHASE PRICE: $

DATE:

COMMENTS:

Please refer to page 166 of brand directory for more information.

ASHTON

Ashtons are medium-bodied cigars made by the same company that produces Arturo Fuente. Created in 1985 by Philadelphia retailer Robert Levin of Holt's, sales of Ashton are about three million per year. In addition to the standard Ashtons, there is a line of Vintage Cabinet cigars, most of which are perfectos, and a series of Aged Maduros, which are particularly limited in supply. Scheduled for launch in 1998 is the Ashton Crown, which will be made with Dominican shade wrappers similar to the Fuente Fuente Opus X.

Manufactured in the Dominican Republic
Fillers/Binders: Dominican Republic
Wrappers: USA/Connecticut Shade

TASTING NOTES

CIGAR PURCHASED:

SIZE:

PLACE PURCHASED:

PURCHASE PRICE: $

DATE:

COMMENTS:

Please refer to page 166 of brand directory for more information.

ASTRAL

Take a billion dollar company, a 25-year history in Honduras, and three years of effort at creating a superpremium brand. The result is Astral, the top-of-the-line cigar from smokeless-tobacco powerhouse UST, which also manufacturers Don Tomas. Made in Danli, Honduras, the key cigar region of that Central American nation, Astrals come in five sizes, including the pyramid-shaped Perfeccion and the unusually formed Favorito, which looks like a reverse pyramid with its tapered foot and normal head.

Manufactured in Honduras
Fillers: Dominican Republic, Nicaragua
Binders: Dominican Republic
Wrappers: Equador

TASTING NOTES

CIGAR PURCHASED:

SIZE:

PLACE PURCHASED:

PURCHASE PRICE: $

DATE:

COMMENTS:

Please refer to page 167 of brand directory for more information.

Avo

Avo is one of the most famous and prestigious brands on the market today, and one
of the biggest success stories in the cigar business. Avo Uvezian and Hendrik Kelner of
Tabacos Dominicanos S.A. created the cigar in
1987, blending Dominican filler and binder
tobaccos with Connecticut shade wrappers.
Sales of Avo—premium-priced from the
start—soared more than tenfold in only three
years, from 20,000 cigars in 1987 to 240,000 in
1990. Today sales are more than 2 million.

Manufactured in the Dominican Republic
Fillers/Binders: Dominican Republic
Wrappers: USA/Connecticut Shade

TASTING NOTES

CIGAR PURCHASED:

SIZE:

PLACE PURCHASED:

PURCHASE PRICE: $

DATE:

COMMENTS:

Please refer to page 167 of brand directory for more information.

BAUZA

When cabdriver Oscar Boruchin picked up a Cuban exile at the Miami airport one day in 1961, it turned out to be the best fare of his life. The man didn't have the money to pay for the ride, so he offered Boruchin a box of Cuban cigars. Boruchin accepted, and that transaction became his unorthodox introduction to selling cigars. Later, he took a sales job with General Cigar Co. and became a partner in Mike's Cigars, a Miami retailer and distributor, in 1981. He acquired the store outright in 1985. In 1990, he acquired the U.S. rights to Bauza. Only about 50,000 Bauzas were sold each year at that time, but Boruchin built it into a national brand, and nearly one million were sold in 1996.

Manufactured in the Dominican Republic
Fillers: Dominican Republic
Binders: Dominican Republic
Wrappers: Ecuador

TASTING NOTES

CIGAR PURCHASED:

SIZE:

PLACE PURCHASED:

PURCHASE PRICE: $

DATE:

COMMENTS:

Please refer to page 167 of brand directory for more information.

BERING

Bering was created in 1905, making it one of the oldest cigar brands in America. Originally a Clear Havana cigar (made in the United States from Cuban tobacco) production of Bering was moved from Tampa, Florida to Honduras in 1990 by Swisher International Group Inc., which bought the brand in 1985. Production is split between Nestor Plasencia and Villazon & Co. Retailing for about $2 each, Berings are among America's most reasonably priced premium cigars. Several sizes are available in double claro (green) wrappers.

Manufactured in Honduras
Fillers: Dominican Republic, Honduras,
   Mexico, Nicaragua
Binders: Honduras
Wrappers: Mexico, USA/Connecticut Shade

TASTING NOTES

CIGAR PURCHASED:

SIZE:

PLACE PURCHASED:

PURCHASE PRICE: $

DATE:

COMMENTS:

Please refer to page 168 of brand directory for more information.

BOLIVAR

Prized for its full, rich flavor, Bolivar is one of Cuba's most powerful brands. Even the smallest cigars in the line, such as the Bonita (4⅞ inches by 40 ring) or the Petit Corona (5 by 42), pack a considerable punch. One of the best in the line is a 5½ inch long, 52 ring gauge torpedo cigar, a Belicoso Fino. The brand gets its name from Simon Bolivar, a strong-willed Venezuelan revolutionary—known as the Liberator—who freed several Latin American countries from Spanish control in the early 1900s. Bolivar was launched in 1901.

Manufactured in Cuba
Fillers/Binders/Wrappers: Cuba

TASTING NOTES

CIGAR PURCHASED:

SIZE:

PLACE PURCHASED:

PURCHASE PRICE: $

DATE:

COMMENTS:

Please refer to page 168 of brand directory for more information.

COHIBA

Cohiba is the most prestigious cigar brand in the world. Created in 1966, the first post-Revolution Cuban cigar was originally the personal cigar of Fidel Castro; the only way to acquire one was as a gift from the Cuban President. Today no other brand carries as high a price tag. Cuba's cigarmakers call Cohiba the selection of the selection, referring to the best filler and binder from Cuba's best tobacco plantations. The brand's distinctive flavor comes from its unique triple fermentation. The Cohiba Robusto is the robusto by which all other Cuban cigars of that size are judged; it is the ultimate accompaniment to a power lunch.

Manufactured in Cuba
Fillers/Binders/Wrappers: Cuba

TASTING NOTES

CIGAR PURCHASED:

SIZE:

PLACE PURCHASED:

PURCHASE PRICE: $

DATE:

COMMENTS:

Please refer to page 170 of brand directory for more information.

CUESTA–REY

In 1884, Angel LaMadrid Cuesta and Peregrino Rey began making cigars in Tampa, Florida. Cuesta-Rey is still going strong as one of the oldest cigar brands in America. M&N Cigar Manufacturers Inc., which also has its roots in the late 1800s, purchased Cuesta-Rey in 1958. In 1986, M&N formed a joint venture with the Fuente family, and began distributing Fuente cigars in the United States. During the 1980s, Fuente began making Cuesta-Rey in the Dominican Republic.

Manufactured in the Dominican Republic
Fillers/Binders: Dominican Republic
Wrappers: Cameroon, USA/Connecticut Shade

TASTING NOTES

CIGAR PURCHASED:

SIZE:

PLACE PURCHASED:

PURCHASE PRICE: $

DATE:

COMMENTS:

Please refer to page 171 of brand directory for more information.

DAVIDOFF

Davidoff cigars were once a Cuban institution. No more. A dispute with Cubatabaco (the former name of Habanos S.A, Cuba's cigar exporting firm) led Davidoff International to take its cigars off the market. But that ending sparked a new beginning. Davidoff cigars were placed in the hands of Hendrik Kelner in the Dominican Republic and the first Dominican-made Davidoffs shipped in November 1990. The cigars are consistently well-made, and among the top-selling brands in the United States; some 6 million were sold in 1996. A 1996 fire claimed the main plant where Davidoffs were made, but production was shifted temporarily, and shipments continue.

Manufactured in the Dominican Republic
Fillers/Binders: Dominican Republic
Wrappers: USA/Connecticut Shade

TASTING NOTES

CIGAR PURCHASED:

SIZE:

PLACE PURCHASED:

PURCHASE PRICE: $

DATE:

COMMENTS:

Please refer to page 171 of brand directory for more information.

DIAMOND CROWN

It's no small feat for a company to reach the ripe old age of 100 years. So when M&N Cigar Manufacturers Inc. was about to hit the century mark, company chairman and patriarch Stanford Newman wanted to celebrate in a big way. Working with the Fuente family, Newman created the Diamond Crown Robusto Series of cigars. Each of the line's five cigars is exceptionally thick, with a 54 ring gauge, but they are surprisingly mellow. Their golden, oily Connecticut shade wrappers are fermented twice. Production is limited to around 200,000 cigars per year.

Manufactured in the Dominican Republic
Fillers/Binders: Dominican Republic
Wrappers: USA/Connecticut Shade

TASTING NOTES

CIGAR PURCHASED:

SIZE:

PLACE PURCHASED:

PURCHASE PRICE: $

DATE:

COMMENTS:

Please refer to page 172 of brand directory for more information.

DON DIEGO

An excellent cigar for beginners, Don Diegos are consistently mild. They were first made in 1962 in the Canary Islands, but today they come from La Romana, Dominican Republic. Don Diego is one of the major brands from Consolidated Cigar. In 1996, Consolidated expanded the line by adding the Playboy by Don Diego cigar, a brand made for the men's magazine *Playboy*. This premium-priced brand is sold in a limited number of shops.

Manufactured in the Dominican Republic
Fillers: Brazil, Dominican Republic
Binders: Dominican Republic
Wrappers: USA/Connecticut Broadleaf,
   USA/Connecticut Shade

TASTING NOTES

CIGAR PURCHASED:

SIZE:

PLACE PURCHASED:

PURCHASE PRICE: $

DATE:

COMMENTS:

Please refer to page 172 of brand directory for more information.

DON TOMAS

This is the original Honduran cigar from UST, the smokeless tobacco company and the maker of Astral. Don Tomas cigars are made in a 25-year-old company factory known as Central American Cigars (CACSA). CACSA is headquartered in Danli, Honduras, a cigar-making haven in the Jalapa Valley running between Nicaragua and Honduras. Don Tomas cigars are rich and flavorful, and are moderately priced.

Manufactured in Honduras
Fillers: Dominican Republic, Mexico, Nicaragua
Binders: Dominican Republic, Mexico
Wrappers: Ecuador, Honduras, Indonesia,
    USA/Connecticut Shade

TASTING NOTES

CIGAR PURCHASED:

SIZE:

PLACE PURCHASED:

PURCHASE PRICE: $

DATE:

COMMENTS:

Please refer to page 173 of brand directory for more information.

DUNHILL AGED CIGARS

Dunhill cigars used to be made in Cuba, but now the brand has been reborn as a Dominican cigar. Dominican Dunhills, made in La Romana by Consolidated Cigar, are created using tobacco from one specific crop. Last year, Dunhill cigars made with tobacco from the 1994 harvest were released by distributor Lane Limited. The first crop released was the 1986, which was followed by 1987 and 1989. Limited stocks of some of the older crops are still on sale. One of the best-known names in cigars, Dunhills are mild- to medium-bodied smokes.

Manufactured in the Dominican Republic
Fillers: Brazil, Dominican Republic
Binders: Dominican Republic
Wrappers: USA/Connecticut Shade

TASTING NOTES

CIGAR PURCHASED:

SIZE:

PLACE PURCHASED:

PURCHASE PRICE: $

DATE:

COMMENTS:

Please refer to page 174 of brand directory for more information.

EL REY DEL MUNDO (HONDURAN)

El Rey del Mundos are rich, spicy cigars made by Villazon & Co. in Honduras. Frank Llaneza, a co-owner of Villazon, is regarded as one of the premier cigar men in the industry. The top cigar from the El Rey del Mundo line, the Flor de Llaneza, is named after him. This flavorful pyramid is not to be missed.

Manufactured in Honduras
Fillers: Dominican Republic, Honduras, Nicaragua
Binders: Honduras
Wrappers: Sumatra

TASTING NOTES

CIGAR PURCHASED:

SIZE:

PLACE PURCHASED:

PURCHASE PRICE: $

DATE:

COMMENTS:

Please refer to page 174 of brand directory for more information.

FONSECA

Originally a Cuban brand created for Spain, Dominican Fonseca cigars are crafted by Manuel (Manolo) Quesada, a man whose great-great grandfather was a tobacco broker in Cuba in the late 1800s. Made with Dominican filler and binders and covered with Connecticut shade wrappers, today's Fonseca cigars have a creamy, smooth flavor. While there are only six sizes in the brand, there is a shape for any time of day, from the diminutive 2-2, which measures 4½ inches by 40 ring gauge, to the 10-10, a 7 inch cigar with a 50 ring gauge. Cuban Fonsecas are still sold outside of the United States.

Manufactured in the Dominican Republic
Fillers: Dominican Republic
Binders: Dominican Republic, Mexico
Wrappers: USA/Connecticut Broadleaf,
    USA/Connecticut Shade

TASTING NOTES

CIGAR PURCHASED: _____

SIZE: _____

PLACE PURCHASED: _____

PURCHASE PRICE: $ _____

DATE: _____

COMMENTS: _____

_____

_____

Please refer to page 175 of brand directory for more information.

FUENTE FUENTE OPUS X

When Carlos Fuente, Jr. planted the seeds that would eventually become the wrappers for Fuente Fuente Opus X cigars, most of his contemporaries in the cigar industry thought the project was a folly. Every company that had tried to grow shade wrappers in the Dominican Republic had failed. But Fuente's family farm yielded dark, superb oily tobacco leaves that would become the hallmark of these rich, flavorful cigars. Made by just a handful of rollers sitting in a special room at one of the Fuente factories, Fuente Fuente Opus X cigars are hard to find. No more than 700,000 were shipped in 1996, and they are only available in about half of the United States.

Manufactured in the Dominican Republic
Fillers/Binders/Wrappers: Dominican Republic

TASTING NOTES

CIGAR PURCHASED: _____

SIZE: _____

PLACE PURCHASED: _____

PURCHASE PRICE: $ _____

DATE: _____

COMMENTS: _____

_____

_____

Please refer to page 176 of brand directory for more information.

H. Upmann (cuban)

Launched 1844, H. Upmann is one of Cuba's oldest brands. The H. Upmann cigar plant, which is now known as José Martí, is widely considered by Cuban cognoscenti to be making the best cigars in Cuba. One of the outstanding cigars in the line is the H. Upmann No. 2, identical in shape to the renowned Montecristo No. 2 pyramid. This exceptional smoke is prized by aficionados for both its quality and its rarity. The H. Upmann factory in Havana makes 15 times more Montecristo No. 2s than Upmann No. 2s in a given year. In 1995, only 60,000 Upmann No. 2s were made.

Manufactured in Cuba
Fillers/Binders/Wrappers: Cuba

Tasting Notes

Cigar Purchased:

Size:

Place Purchased:

Purchase Price: $

Date:

Comments:

Please refer to page 176 of brand directory for more information.

H. UPMANN (DOMINICAN)

The popularity of Dominican H. Upmanns has surged in recent years. They are the flagship brand of Consolidated Cigar, and the company sold around nine million cigars in 1996, making it one of the biggest brands in the United States. While the traditional H. Upmann line is moderately priced, the brand has been expanded to include the H. Upmann Chairman's Reserve, cigars that are made with the personal blend of tobaccos smoked by billionaire Ronald O. Perelman, the chairman of Consolidated. They are available only in a small number of shops.

Manufactured in the Dominican Republic
Fillers: Brazil, Dominican Republic
Binders: Dominican Republic
Wrappers: Cameroon, Indonesia

TASTING NOTES

CIGAR PURCHASED:

SIZE:

PLACE PURCHASED:

PURCHASE PRICE: $

DATE:

COMMENTS:

Please refer to page 176 of brand directory for more information.

HOYO DE MONTERREY (CUBAN)

This venerable Cuban brand was launched in 1865. Many cigar lovers consider the Hoyo de Monterrey Double Corona to be the world's finest cigar. With its reddish, dark wrapper seeping with oils and its seemingly endless layers of rich flavor, the cigar is a masterpiece. It is nearly impossible to find. Other Hoyos are highly regarded as well, such as the Le Hoyo series of cigars in cabinets, which are richer than the rest of the line, and the Epicure Nos. 1 and 2, a great corona gorda and a classic robusto.

Fillers/Binders/Wrappers: Cuba

TASTING NOTES

CIGAR PURCHASED:

SIZE:

PLACE PURCHASED:

PURCHASE PRICE: $

DATE:

COMMENTS:

Please refer to page 177 of brand directory for more information.

HOYO DE MONTERREY
AND
HOYO DE MONTERREY
EXCALIBUR (HONDURAN)

The non-Cuban version of Hoyo de Monterrey was born in a Tampa cigar factory in 1965. But when their aging Florida workforce died out, the brand owners, Dan Blumenthal and Frank Llaneza, moved production to Honduras. Named after the legendary Cuban brand, this is a rich, moderately priced cigar that comes in a variety of sizes, including the rare culebra. The Excalibur series (sold simply as the Excalibur outside the U.S. due to trademark conflicts) is the premier line from Hoyo, made with top-quality Connecticut shade wrappers.

Manufactured in Honduras
Fillers: Dominican Republic, Honduras, Nicaragua
Binders: Honduras, Nicaragua
Wrappers: Ecuador, Sumatra, USA/Connecticut
   Broadleaf, USA/Connecticut Shade

TASTING NOTES

CIGAR PURCHASED:

SIZE:

PLACE PURCHASED:

PURCHASE PRICE: $

DATE:

COMMENTS:

Please refer to page 178 of brand directory for more information.

JOYA DE NICARAGUA

In the 1970s and early 1980s, Nicaraguan cigars were among the finest in the world; it was even rumored that Cuba was using Nicaraguan wrappers on some of its cigars. But civil war between the Contras and Sandinistas laid waste to this Central American nation's cigar industry. Factories were bombed and fields were destroyed. During the war years, the United States stopped trading with Nicaragua, and the cigars disappeared from the market from 1981 to 1990. But peace has returned to Nicaragua, and its cigars have made a comeback. Shipments of the nation's premier brand, Joya de Nicaragua—once nearly 3 million per year—have grown back to around 1.4 million per year, and the cigars have improved noticeably, hinting at a return to past quality.

Manufactured in Nicaragua
Fillers/Binders: Nicaragua
Wrappers: Costa Rica, Ecuador, Nicaragua

TASTING NOTES

CIGAR PURCHASED:

SIZE:

PLACE PURCHASED:

PURCHASE PRICE: $

DATE:

COMMENTS:

Please refer to page 179 of brand directory for more information.

LA AURORA

When Eduardo Leon Jimenes created a cigar factory in the Cibao Valley of the Dominican Republic in 1903, few could imagine that it would one day grow into the Dominican giant Empresas Leon Jimenes. Relocated to Santiago in 1937, this company now controls 98 percent of the Dominican beer market, 89 percent of the nation's cigarette market, and 50 percent of its local cigar market. La Aurora is its key cigar brand. Made with Dominican tobaccos and a Cameroon wrapper, it was first exported to the United States in the 1950s. The company also makes Leon Jimenes cigars, which have Connecticut shade wrappers. Today Guillermo Leon supervises cigar production, following in the ways of his grandfather.

Manufactured in the Dominican Republic
Fillers: Dominican Republic
Binders: Dominican Republic, Sumatra
Wrappers: Cameroon, USA/Connecticut Broadleaf

TASTING NOTES

CIGAR PURCHASED:

SIZE:

PLACE PURCHASED:

PURCHASE PRICE: $

DATE:

COMMENTS:

Please refer to page 180 of brand directory for more information.

LA GLORIA CUBANA

Before 1992, few cigar smokers knew the name La Gloria Cubana. Miami cigar-maker Ernesto Perez-Carrillo made a few hundred thousand cigars a year, sold them to Miami locals, and charged about a dollar per cigar. Today Carrillo's powerful, full-bodied cigars—made with a blend of tobaccos from several countries and covered with oily Ecuador wrappers—are in strong demand. He recently opened a new plant in the Dominican Republic. Cuban La Gloria Cubanas are still manufactured in Havana.

Manufactured in the Dominican Republic
  and Florida
Fillers: Brazil, Dominican Republic, Mexico,
  Nicaragua
Binders: Dominican Republic, Ecuador, Nicaragua
Wrappers: Ecuador

TASTING NOTES

CIGAR PURCHASED:

SIZE:

PLACE PURCHASED:

PURCHASE PRICE: $

DATE:

COMMENTS:

Please refer to page 181 of brand directory for more information.

LICENCIADOS

Retailer and distributor Oscar Boruchin of Miami's Mike's Cigars joined with cigarmaker Manuel Quesada of Manufactura de Tabacos S.A. to create Licenciados in 1987. They blended Dominican filler with a Honduran binder and a Connecticut shade wrapper for a medium-bodied, smooth smoke. Today Licenciados sales are approaching one million cigars.

Manufactured in the Dominican Republic
Fillers: Dominican Republic
Binders: Dominican Republic, Honduras
Wrappers: USA/Connecticut Broadleaf,
  USA/Connecticut Shade

TASTING NOTES

CIGAR PURCHASED:

SIZE:

PLACE PURCHASED:

PURCHASE PRICE: $

DATE:

COMMENTS:

Please refer to page 182 of brand directory for more information.

MACANUDO

Prized for their consistency, smooth taste and medium-bodied flavors, Macanudos are the best selling premium cigars in the United States. They are ideally suited to beginning cigar smokers, and come in a wide array of sizes. Created by Edgar M. Cullman, the chairman of General Cigar, most are made in Jamaica, with around 10 percent rolled in the Dominican Republic. The wrappers are grown on farms owned by General in Connecticut, and they are aged twice for extra smoothness. The Hyde Park, a corona gorda size, is flawlessly constructed, with smooth, creamy flavors. The Macanudo Vintage line, declared when a particularly good crop is in the barns, is both rich tasting and premium priced.

Manufactured in the Dominican Republic
    and Jamaica
Fillers: Dominican Republic, Mexico/San Andreas
Binders: Mexico/San Andreas
Wrappers: USA/Connecticut Shade

TASTING NOTES

CIGAR PURCHASED:

SIZE:

PLACE PURCHASED:

PURCHASE PRICE: $

DATE:

COMMENTS:

Please refer to page 183 of brand directory for more information.

MONTECRISTO
(CUBAN)

Montecristo is, hands down, Cuba's best-selling cigar brand. The Montecristo No. 4 alone makes up nearly half of all Cuban cigar exports in any given year. These petit coronas are ubiquitous in international cigar stores. Among big cigars, it's hard to find a more impressive smoke than a Montecristo A, a 9½ inch, 47 ring gauge cigar. The Montecristo No. 2, the pyramid by which all other pyramids are measured, is a cigar without peer. It is packed with layers of leathery, rich flavors.

Manufactured in Cuba
Fillers/Binders/Wrappers: Cuba

TASTING NOTES

CIGAR PURCHASED:

SIZE:

PLACE PURCHASED:

PURCHASE PRICE: $

DATE:

COMMENTS:

Please refer to page 184 of brand directory for more information.

MONTECRISTO
(DOMINICAN)

Unlike its sister Cuban brand, Dominican Montecristos are not made in great quantity. While production doubled in 1996, it grew to only 1 million cigars. But while Montecristo may be one of the nation's smaller cigar brands, demand is exceptional. These are well-made, medium-bodied cigars; the names and shapes are similar to the Cuban line, with some exceptions. The No. 2 is formed a bit differently than the Cuban Montecristo No. 2, and the Dominican brand features a robusto and a Churchill, which the Cuban line doesn't offer.

Manufactured in the Dominican Republic
Fillers/Binders: Dominican Republic
Wrappers: USA/Connecticut Shade

TASTING NOTES

CIGAR PURCHASED:

SIZE:

PLACE PURCHASED:

PURCHASE PRICE: $

DATE:

COMMENTS:

Please refer to page 184 of brand directory for more information.

PADRÓN

The Padrón family has worked tobacco since the late 1800s. In 1964 Jose O. Padrón, who was born on a Cuban tobacco farm to a family of leaf growers, began rolling cigars from Nicaraguan tobacco in Miami. Padrón moved its manufacturing operations to Nicaragua in 1970, and added a Honduran plant in 1978. In 1994, the company commemorated its 30th anniversary with a new line of exceptional, specially aged and box-pressed cigars called Padrón 1964 Anniversary Series.

Manufactured in Honduras and Nicaragua
Fillers/Binders/Wrappers: Nicaragua

TASTING NOTES

CIGAR PURCHASED:

SIZE:

PLACE PURCHASED:

PURCHASE PRICE: $

DATE:

COMMENTS:

Please refer to page 186 of brand directory for more information.

PARTAGAS (CUBAN)

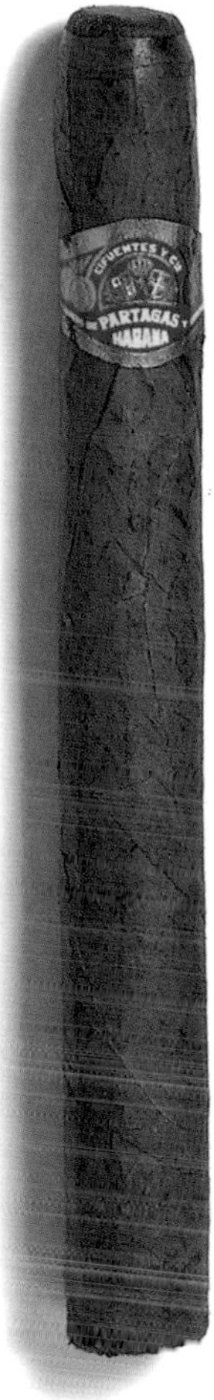

Partagas is one of the oldest cigar brands in the world, having turned 150 in 1995. Known for its full flavor, it is one of Cuba's most popular cigars. The Partagas factory in downtown Havana also has claim as the most famous cigar-making facility in Cuba. Renamed Francisco Perez German after the Cuban Revolution, it is the one Cuban cigar plant that can be toured by the public.

To celebrate its sesquicentennial, Habanos S.A. created 150 numbered humidors, each packed with 150 Partagas cigars: 50 Serie D No. 4 Robustos, 50 8-9-8s, and 50 specially tapered Lusitanias, the rare and prized double corona from Partagas.

Manufactured in Cuba
Fillers/Binders/Wrappers: Cuba

TASTING NOTES

CIGAR PURCHASED:

SIZE:

PLACE PURCHASED:

PURCHASE PRICE: $

DATE:

COMMENTS:

Please refer to page 186 of brand directory for more information.

71

PARTAGAS (DOMINICAN)

Dominican Partagas is one of the best-selling cigars in the United States. General Cigar began production of this parallel brand after acquiring the rights from Ramon Cifuentes, who made Partagas cigars in Cuba before fleeing after the Revolution. One of the classic cigars of the world is the Partagas No. 10, a double corona with a rich, dark wrapper. When Partagas turned 150 years old, General Cigar created a 150 Signature Series cigar made with 18-year-old Cameroon wrapper leaf to commemorate the historic event. The company also occasionally releases Partagas Limited Reserve cigars.

Manufactured in the Dominican Republic
Fillers: Dominican Republic, Mexico/San Andreas
Binders: Mexico/San Andreas
Wrappers: Cameroon

TASTING NOTES

CIGAR PURCHASED:

SIZE:

PLACE PURCHASED:

PURCHASE PRICE: $

DATE:

COMMENTS:

Please refer to page 187 of brand directory for more information.

PUNCH (CUBAN)

Created by Don Manuel Lopez in 1840 for the British export market, Punch is known for having an excellent range of flavors without being overpowering. Punch delivers superb quality. There are several excellent large cigars in the line, such as the Punch Double Corona and the Punch Churchill. Both are world-class smokes. The Punch Punch corona gorda is a classic cigar of that size.

Manufactured in Cuba
Fillers/Binders/Wrappers: Cuba

TASTING NOTES

CIGAR PURCHASED:

SIZE:

PLACE PURCHASED:

PURCHASE PRICE: $

DATE:

COMMENTS:

Please refer to page 189 of brand directory for more information.

PUNCH (HONDURAN)

Originally made in Tampa, production of this brand (as well as Hoyo de Monterrey) was shifted to Honduras in 1969. It was one of the first brands to be made in that country. Today, Honduras is a major cigar-making country, second only to the Dominican Republic in terms of exports of premium cigars to the United States. The Rothschild, which has a suggested retail price of $2.15, is one of the premier bargains in handmade cigars.

Manufactured in Honduras
Fillers: Dominican Republic, Honduras, Nicaragua
Binders: Ecuador, Honduras
Wrappers: Ecuador, Honduras, USA/Connecticut
    Broadleaf, USA/Connecticut Shade

TASTING NOTES

CIGAR PURCHASED:

SIZE:

PLACE PURCHASED:

PURCHASE PRICE: $

DATE:

COMMENTS:

Please refer to page 189 of brand directory for more information.

RAMON ALLONES
(CUBAN)

R amon Allones is one of Cuba's smallest exported brands, but it is well-known to aficionados of Cuban cigars, who look to the brand for its intensity of flavors and full-bodied character. Two of the sizes in this line are among the best of their size anywhere. The double corona Gigantes, if you can find it, is an exquisite smoke. Loaded with flavors, it still remains refined. The Specially Selected robusto is another classic cigar that shouldn't be missed.

Manufactured in Cuba
Fillers/Binders/Wrappers: Cuba

TASTING NOTES

CIGAR PURCHASED:

SIZE:

PLACE PURCHASED:

PURCHASE PRICE: $

DATE:

COMMENTS:

Please refer to page 190 of brand directory for more information.

ROMEO Y JULIETA
(CUBAN)

Romeo y Julieta ranks among Cuba's most sought-after brands. One of the best sizes in the line is the Churchill. Named by the Romeo y Julieta factory in honor of Sir Winston Churchill, one of history's greatest cigar smokers, this 7 inch by 47 ring cigar is immensely flavorful and well made—the Churchill by which all other cigars of that size are measured. While the Romeo line is vast, not all are premium cigars. Note that cigars with a number in their name are machine-made unless they are designated as deluxe. Thus Romeo No. 1 is a machine-made cigar, while the Romeo No. 1 de Luxe is handmade.

Manufactured in Cuba
Fillers/Binders/Wrappers: Cuba

TASTING NOTES

CIGAR PURCHASED:

SIZE:

PLACE PURCHASED:

PURCHASE PRICE: $

DATE:

COMMENTS:

Please refer to page 191 of brand directory for more information.

ROMEO Y JULIETA
(DOMINICAN)

Carefully crafted in the Dominican Republic by Manuel Quesada of Manufactura de Tabacos S.A. de C.V. (MATASA), Romeo y Julietas are some of the most difficult cigars to find. Prized for their smooth, creamy flavors and excellent construction, only about 700,000 of these medium-bodied cigars are made each year, but the brand has back orders of five million cigars.

Manufactured in the Dominican Republic
Fillers: Brazil, Dominican Republic
Binders: Mexico, USA/Connecticut Broadleaf
Wrappers: Cameroon, Indonesia,
    USA/Connecticut Shade

TASTING NOTES

CIGAR PURCHASED:

SIZE:

PLACE PURCHASED:

PURCHASE PRICE: $

DATE:

COMMENTS:

Please refer to page 191 of brand directory for more information.

ROYAL JAMAICA

Royal Jamaica cigars used to be made in Jamaica. Hurricane Gilbert ended that affair, tearing the roof off of the cigar factory in 1988. Production of the brand was shifted to the Dominican Republic, where it remained until late 1996. But then Consolidated Cigar opened a new cigar plant in Jamaica, and the first Royal Jamaicas from that factory arrived in the U.S. in 1997. Most handmade cigars are flavored only with different blends of tobacco, but Royal Jamaicas owe their distinctive taste to a concoction of Jamaican rum and boiled Jamaican herbs known as bethune that is sprayed on the filler tobacco during the curing process.

Manufactured in Jamaica
Fillers: Dominican Republic, Indonesia, Jamaica
Binders: Cameroon, Indonesia
Wrappers: Cameroon, Indonesia, Mexico

TASTING NOTES

CIGAR PURCHASED:

SIZE:

PLACE PURCHASED:

PURCHASE PRICE: $

DATE:

COMMENTS:

Please refer to page 191 of brand directory for more information.

SIGNATURE COLLECTION BY SANTIAGO CABANA

Kevin Doyle was an air traffic controller and a cigar lover. On a lark, he opened a small cigar store in the Florida Keys in 1994, and met a Cuban cigar roller named Santiago Cabana. Doyle hired the man to roll cigars in his store, and customers began flowing in. From that small start, Doyle created a growing company that now manufactures, distributes, and retails the cigars. Doyle took his small company public in 1996, becoming, at the time, the first public company with a business focused solely on cigars. His Signature Collection by Santiago Cabana cigars are medium-bodied, and the torpedo is an exceptional smoke.

Manufactured in Florida
Fillers: Dominican Republic, Honduras, Nicaragua
Binders/Wrappers: Ecuador

TASTING NOTES

CIGAR PURCHASED:

SIZE:

PLACE PURCHASED:

PURCHASE PRICE: $

DATE:

COMMENTS:

Please refer to page 193 of brand directory for more information.

TE–AMO

Known for its earthy flavor and extremely reasonable price, Te-Amos are not only the best-selling Mexican cigar in America, but one of the top brands overall. A staple of the New York market since its inception, the Te-Amo has spread across the United States, and distributor Consolidated Cigar sold around 9 million in 1996. A Mexican puro, made entirely from Mexican tobaccos, Te-Amos have a distinctive taste and a rather rustic appearance. They are made in nearly every size imaginable, including several figurados that are full flavored. The new double perfecto is especially well made.

Manufactured in Mexico
Fillers/Binders/Wrappers: Mexico

TASTING NOTES

CIGAR PURCHASED:

SIZE:

PLACE PURCHASED:

PURCHASE PRICE: $

DATE:

COMMENTS:

Please refer to page 193 of brand directory for more information.

ZINO

Zino cigars are named after the premier elder statesman of the cigar world, the late Zino Davidoff. The Zino cigar is made in Honduras, from Honduran fillers and binders and Ecuador wrappers. It is a medium-bodied cigar. The Mouton-Cadet line, created and launched jointly with the Baron Phillipe de Rothschild in 1983, features a Connecticut shade wrapper. The Zino line was one of the first superpremium cigar lines in the United States.

Manufactured in Honduras
Fillers/Binders: Honduras
Wrappers: Ecuador, Honduras,
   USA/Connecticut Shade

TASTING NOTES

CIGAR PURCHASED: _____

SIZE: _____

PLACE PURCHASED: _____

PURCHASE PRICE: $ _____

DATE: _____

COMMENTS: _____

_____

_____

Please refer to page 196 of brand directory for more information.

CHAPTER 4

PREPARING TO SMOKE: CUTTING AND LIGHTING YOUR CIGAR

The Tricks of the Trade

Preparing to smoke a cigar can be a wonderful experience in itself. You will be spending quality time with a quality product, and it will be to your benefit to reflect upon its creation before lighting up. Unlike cigarettes, you do not simply pull out a cigar, light the tip, and start puffing. First of all, almost every premium cigar has a closed head that must be cut before you can begin to smoke. Also, you would do well to use something other than a paper match for your source of ignition. There are several ways to cut a cigar, the best being what suits the individual. However, there is only one way to effectively light a cigar.

Cutting Your Cigar

Watch the actors in old movies and you'll see that there is a host of ways to open the closed end of a cigar before smoking it. Some characters used a pocketknife to cut a neat V-shaped notch. Others used horseshoe nails as piercers. Certain film stars in tough-guy roles bit off the end and spat it out. Some people today still use these methods but, for the most part, cutting cigars has become a bit less colorful and a bit more elegant.

The better the cigars you smoke, the more attention you'll want to pay to the cut. A bad cut will ruin a cigar.

The object of the cut is to create an ample, smooth opening for smoking without damaging the cigar's structure. With most cigars, this means cutting away part of the cap or flag leaf that closes the cigar, while leaving some of it glued around the end to keep the filler leaves together. If you are making a wedge cut or a bull's-eye cut, be careful not to penetrate too deeply into the cigar. You want to create a large, exposed surface of cleanly-cut filler leaves which will allow equal draw from the core and the rim of the cigar.

On most cigars, you'll want to make the cut about one-sixteenth of an inch (about two millimeters) from the end. When you aren't carrying a precision measuring device, you can simply look for the shoulder—the place where the curved end of the cigar starts to straighten out—and make your cut there.

Another alternative is to make a V-shaped wedge cut in the end of the cigar. This style of cut exposes a lot of surface area and makes it easy to draw smoke through the cigar. Unfortunately, the draw is sometimes too good and the cigar will smoke too hot. Wedge cuts are a particularly bad idea for people who tend to chew their cigars. If they chomp down hard enough while the wedge is horizontal, the opening may collapse and tear the structure of the cigar, closing off the draw.

Cutting Tools

There are a number of devices which will help you cut your cigar in a single, swift motion that minimizes the chance of tearing the wrapper. Many aficionados have several cutters, from compact wafer-thin cutters that nestle in a pocket to more massive cutters that are less likely to be misplaced.

Suggested strategy: buy yourself your first cutter and drop gift hints for the rest. Engraved initials make sure that valuable cutters find their way back to you after they have been borrowed.

Of course, you already have a set of cutters: your teeth. But there are a few drawbacks to the biting method. First of all, it's hard to see what you're doing. Secondly, your teeth aren't as sharp as a cutter's razor blade. And thirdly, you end up with an unsightly wad of tobacco in your mouth.

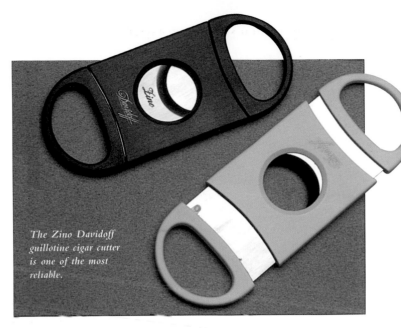

The Zino Davidoff guillotine cigar cutter is one of the most reliable.

Knives, on the other hand, are easy to keep sharp. But it takes great skill and very steady hands to cut cigars properly with a knife. If you do choose this method, you'll want to avoid cleansing your pocketknife with oils, which may pollute your cigar.

Piercers—sometimes called lances—are intriguing, but hard to use. If a cigar is pierced too deeply, a tunnel may form that causes the center of the cigar to burn too hot. Moreover, the area opened by piercing has two drawbacks: 1) the smoker may get an uneven draw which minimizes the intended effect of blending different leaves into the bunch to create unique flavors; 2) since tars and nicotine tend to accumulate at the openings that channel the smoke, the small hole produced by a piercer will likely concentrate these nasty substances even further, sending more of them into the smoker's mouth and air passages.

Double- and single-bladed pocket cutters, scissors, and desk-top devices are designed to make a cut across the end of the cigar. These are generally the best options.

When you are using a single-bladed cutter, the cigar should be placed against the far side of the opening—away from the blade—and the blade brought down to touch the cigar before you make the cutting stroke. This keeps the cigar properly positioned and prevents motion which might lead to tearing or to the cut happening in the wrong place. Once the cigar is in position, cut it boldly using swift, even pressure. A true aficionado cuts like a surgeon: quickly and confidently.

With single-bladed cutters it is important to make sure the compartment that sheaths the blade doesn't fill up with bits of tobacco. This will gum up the works and impede quick, clean cuts. All cutters should be kept as sharp as possible. Note that it is more difficult to sharpen some of the smaller, more intricate cutters.

The advantage of double-bladed or guillotine cutters is that the cutting proceeds from both sides simultaneously. There is less chance that the cigar wrapper will be torn since it is not being pushed against a non-sharp surface. Again, the technique is to rest the cigar against a blade before clicking the cutter shut.

Special cigar-cutting scissors can make extremely clean cuts

Invest in a cutter that will create an ample, smooth opening without damaging the cigar's structure. Above, cutter by Dunhill.

and are an elegant accessory, but they must be wielded with some care. The fit and balance of cigar scissors is as important and as unique to an individual as that of golf clubs. Try out a pair before investing in them. They should balance easily in one hand so that you'll be able to hold them steady through the cutting motion while you hold a cigar in the other hand. If the handles and blades don't balance with each other when you hold them, the scissors aren't for you. Also, if the hinge is placed so that you cannot move your fingers without stretching past your hand's normal span, then try another pair.

It's worth investing in a good cutter. Remember that a bad cut will ruin a good cigar, and it doesn't take a lot of ruined cigars to add up to the cost of even a very elegant cutter.

How to Light a Cigar

Lighting a cigar is not like lighting the tip of a cigarette or the wick of a candle—it takes longer. Light your cigar the same way you would toast a marshmallow over a campfire—keep the cigar above and near the flame, but don't let them touch. Burning a cigar directly in a flame makes it too hot. And, as with a marshmallow, you'll want to rotate the cigar so all parts of its tip are equally heated. Be patient and keep at it until there's a glowing ring all the way around the cigar's tip. Once the cigar is lit, gently blow on the embers to create a smooth, completely rounded ash.

Then, raise the unlit end of the cigar to your mouth and take the first puff. Many aficionados blow the first puff out through the cigar in order to avoid unsavory flavors such as sulfur from matches or gases from lighters. No one, of course, should ever apply more than one outward puff.

To Relight, or Not to Relight

Some purists think that it's shameful to ever have to relight a cigar. Realistically, even the best cigars will go out on those occasions when the conversation becomes so absorbing that

Cigar lighters that have a large flame are most likely to furnish an even light.

you forget to take a puff for a couple of minutes. It's no worse to have to relight a cigar than it is to have to fish a bit of cork out of a fine glass of wine. It will generally take you less time to relight an already-warm cigar than it does to light one for the first time.

Do not, however, intentionally let your cigar die out and then relight it the next day. This will lead to stale, harsh flavors which will ruin your fine memories of the first few puffs.

If you have to relight a cigar several times, you may have a badly-rolled cigar. Premium cigars are made by hand, not by machine, and they are made from organic materials which retain much of their natural, irregular structure and character. Despite dedicated quality control efforts, a substandard cigar occasionally makes its way to the market. Don't hesitate to bring a badly rolled cigar back to your tobacconist. Most will happily replace it.

Choosing Your Flame

Never light a cigar with a flame from a source that will alter the essence of your cigar. Using a candle, for example, is a temptingly theatrical gesture, but the burning candlewax can add an odd flavor to your cigar. So can the fluid from an iso-butane cigarette lighter. Many smokers also object to the sulfur used in most match tips.

If you insist on using a candle or a fluid lighter, use it to light a strip of cedar, called a spill, and use that to light the cigar. If you insist on matches, try to get extra-long, wooden sulfurless ones. If you can't find them and are using regular, short matches, be prepared to use a number of them. Be sure to let the sulfur burn off before starting the lighting process and try lighting two at a time, so you get a broader flame.

Cigar lighters are the easiest way to get an even light. What makes a lighter a *cigar* lighter? First of all, a cigar lighter uses odorless gas. Cigar lighters often have "fatter" flames, or even two adjacent flame sources, and adjustable flame heights.

Cigar lighters come in a wide range of designs and materi-als, so it will be easy to find one that's an appropriate accessory for your sense of style. Your first requirement should, of course, be performance. A good lighter, like a good pen, should fit your hand. The cap should open easily and swing back so the whole flame is available for lighting.

CHAPTER 5

ETIQUETTE TIPS

The Keys to Cultured Smoking

I t is a cruel irony that those of us who appreciate premium cigars and who tend to be among the most cultured of people are so frequently labeled "boorish." Becoming a true aficionado involves learning how to prevent these criticisms by showing some basic consideration for other smokers and non-smokers. At the same time, you want to be sure to maintain your integrity as a cigar smoker and guard your right to smoke.

Among Non Smokers

To begin with, only share your cigar smoke with those who appreciate it. The company of fellow aficionados will enhance your pleasure; the company of people intent on harping at you will not. Consult the list of cigar-friendly restaurants in *Cigar Aficionado's* annual *Buying Guide* and on the *Cigar Aficionado* website at http://www.cigaraficionado.com, or the list of establishments hosting Smoker Nights in the magazine itself, so you'll know where to find restaurants that encourage you to casually indulge yourself.

Don't smoke in elevators, vestibules, or other confined spaces. Even if you are smoking in a well ventilated public place where smoking is permitted and someone politely complains, it may be easier for you to move than to assert your rights.

Conscientious smokers do their best to minimize the criticism they receive from others. Their homes tend to be well-ventilated to start with, and they are fanatical about throwing out stubs and ashes rather than leaving them around a room

until they develop a stale reek. The same, incidentally, goes for wine drinkers. Avid wine appreciators empty every glass in the room (into themselves or the sink) before going to bed.

Similarly, true cigar aficionados have their clothes—particularly their tweeds—cleaned frequently. Fresh cigars in a case in your pocket may exude a slight, tantalizing aroma, but they do not emit the harsh personal atmosphere that makes people suspect that you are a chimney sweep or a firefighter.

In the Company of Aficionados

When you are safely surrounded by other eager smokers, you are faced with a new set of etiquette challenges:

Sharing. Although cigar smokers are generally well-mannered people, you are not expected to bring enough to share with everyone. In fact, if you are in a store, restaurant, club, or other establishment that sells cigars, it is inconsiderate to pass out "freebies."

The cigar band. Do whatever you like: remove it or leave it on. There is no rule. Note, however, that many aficionados leave their cigar bands on—it tells others a bit about yourself and often sparks engaging discussions.

The smoke. Exhale smoke away from other people, even aficionados. Blowing smoke into someone's face is nothing less than confrontational.

Cutters and lighters. Immediately return any lighters or cutters that you borrow. "I forgot" is never an acceptable excuse.

Cutting. Don't cut another person's cigar without asking. Cutting cigars for a guest or friend seems like a friendly gesture, but it's not always welcome. Cutting a cigar is a very personal ritual for many people, and cutting their cigar uninvited is like driving their car uninvited (and adjusting the seat while you're at it)—it violates personal territory. Some people swear by the easy draw of V-wedge cuts; other people think these cuts are an abomination.

Lighting. Don't help someone light a cigar without asking. Lighting a cigar is as personal as cutting one. Some aficionados feel it's criminal to light a cigar without warming it over a match or lighter first, to encourage it to ignite and draw properly. Others find this foreplay not only unnecessary, but even potentially damaging to their perfectly humidified cigars.

If you are going to help someone light a cigar, be careful of the flame. The procedure of lighting a cigar often causes the flame to jump; it's all too easy to singe bangs, beards, and eye brows. And, while Claude Rains managed to look classy while lighting two cigarettes at once in *Now Voyager*, it's not a good trick to try with cigars. They each deserve individual attention.

Women. Don't assume a woman needs to be educated about cigars. There are a surprising number of women out there who learned all about cigars from their fathers (or mothers), and even a few whose families have been in the cigar business for generations. They could teach many smokers a thing or two about tobacco.

Humidors *(see next chapter)*. Never take from a humidor without being invited to do so. Friends have fallen out over this issue. You may be welcome to raid the refrigerator. You may even be expected to help yourself to the Cognac. But pillaging the humidor is a different matter—more like picking flowers from a carefully laid-out garden. Did you take the one that he's promised to smoke at his partner's funeral? Did you ruin his count so he now suspects his golf buddy of "borrowing?" Did you get a cigar that he's spent the last month carefully moving toward the middle of the humidor in order to restore it to smokability? Treat humidors with the same respect and discretion you would use for a personal diary or a safe-deposit box.

Never take more than one. In cigar circles, "help yourself" means "take one." Don't load your pockets, unless specifically encouraged to do so.

Experiment. If you are lucky enough to travel to one of the many places where cigars are made, it's only polite to try the local product, even if you already have a favorite. You may discover something marvelous. If you do, find out if it's legal to bring a few back to share with friends.

Births. Celebrate the birth of both girls and boys by passing out cigars. Some people still save the cigars for the appearance of a boy. I, however, hope you're just as happy to

have a girl—and you will need just as many friends to help raise the child. Pass them out to show your pride.

Pranks. Exploding cigars are not humorous. They are very dangerous and, because of this, they're just not funny. Don't hand them out, and don't associate with anyone who does.

At Celebrations

Cigars are one of the rewards in life. Here are some times when it is particularly appropriate not only to reward yourself, but also to present cigars to a close friend or two who will appreciate them:

- Birth of a child
- Wedding
- Closing a business deal
- Retirement
- Holiday

- Founding of a company
- Graduation
- Promotion
- Birthday
- Sports victory

In Times of Sorrow

While nearly everyone recognizes cigars' appropriateness for celebrations, a civilized few have realized how helpful they can be at times of great loss. At moments when almost any words would seem shallow and inappropriate, a cigar may offer the perfect excuse for wordless, meditative communion and fellowship. It's as appropriate to carry cigars to a memorial service as it is to tuck an extra handkerchief into a pocket.

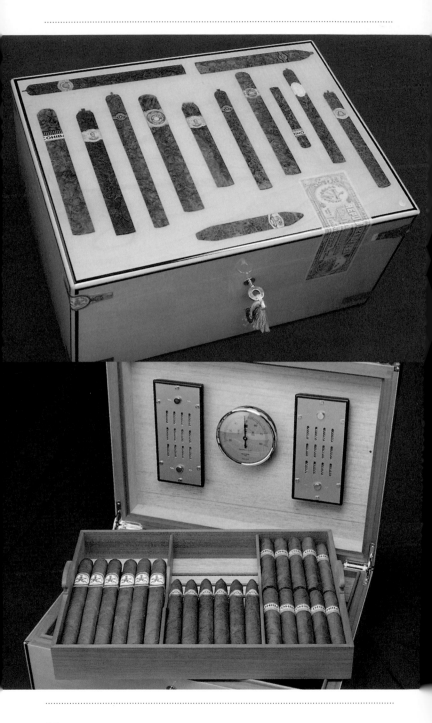

CHAPTER 6
STORING CIGARS
Protect Your Collection

In many ways, fine cigars are like wine, orchids, or humans traveling in space. They are natural, organic, and sensitive to their environment. They are the mature products of a carefully controlled combination of temperature and moisture.

The first thing to know is that cigars should stay in a humidor—pronounced: HUE-mih-dor until they're ready to be smoked. When necessary, you can get away with keeping properly humidified cigars in a sealed plastic bag with a small, damp paper towel for a day or so. But, if you want to become a true aficionado, a humidor is an essential piece of equipment.

A humidor is an elegantly simple device that keeps cigars at their best by maintaining them in conditions similar to those in which their tobacco grew, fermented, and was rolled.

Left out in a heated or air conditioned room, a cigar can dry out and die as quickly as the most delicate flower— in less than an hour. In a properly maintained humidor—the atmosphere inside of which closely mimics that of a tropical isle—cigars can be kept for years.

Dedicated aficionados often have more than one humidor. Perhaps a large one that stays at home, and a smaller, more portable one that holds a day or two's supply. Some aficionados even keep different humidors for different brands of cigars. Within a humidor, the scents from various cigars mingle or "marry," and subtle shifts in flavor can result from cigars of one sort being stored adjacent to very different ones.

Many cigars are packaged in cellophane. Before putting the cigars in your humidor for aging, the cellophane wrapper should be removed so that the individual cigar can breathe.

Davidoff

A humidor is, quite simply, a storage container designed to allow minimal air flow and equipped with a device that maintains an internal humidity in the range of 70–72 percent and an internal temperature in a narrow range of about 68–70 degrees Fahrenheit. (Without the device to maintain the internal humidity, it's not a humidor—it's just a box.) Humidors come in all sizes. Travel-sized humidors hold just a few cigars; room-sized humidors hold thousands of boxes of cigars.

Note that a humidor is not a sealed environment. Inside a totally airtight, moisturized container, cigars are likely to become moldy. For that reason, it's better to have air circulating between the cigars in your humidor than it is to squeeze them in too tightly. Besides, tightly packed cigars can become box-pressed, taking on a slightly squarish appearance.

While a humidor needs a device which maintains moisture levels, it does not necessarily need a gauge. Some humidors, however, come with hygrometers which indicate the interior humidity. While the analog models often have the appealing style of a dial on a sports car's dashboard, they are frequently inaccurate. Digital read–out hygrometers are usually reliable to a level of plus or minus two percent.

No matter what a thermometer or hygrometer says, the true measure of your humidor's performance will be the condition of the cigars inside of it. If the cigars are exuding a little oil, the conditions are perfect. If they seem too dry, you should add more water. If they turn moldy, you will—probably with a tear or two in your eye—have to throw out the cigars, no matter what the hygrometer says. There's even a species of beetle which occasionally ruins the contents of humidors, but only humidors which maintain a temperature above 75° for more than 24 hours. If your humidor becomes afflicted by these insects, freeze the contaminated cigars for 48 hours, then refrigerate them for 24 hours. The beetles and larvae will not survive.

Maintaining a Humidor

Humidors are much simpler to maintain than other balanced environments, such as tropical fish tanks. All you have to do is keep the lid or door shut and periodically add distilled water to the humidifying device. (If you use regular tap water, the minerals in it are likely to collect on the humidifier and diminish its ability to emit and absorb moisture.)

Michel Perrenoud

A little common sense helps, too. Placing a humidor in direct, broiling sunlight is almost inviting the humidor to warp. And locating it on top of an air conditioner or radiator is asking a humidifier to work harder than it should have to. Leaving a travel humidor on the exposed back window deck of a car also creates the risk of theft, as well as warping.

Selecting Your Humidor

Investing in a humidor requires careful thought. The bad news is that good humidors are relatively expensive. There's no point in having a bad humidor. A humidor that does not maintain a constant tropical humidity and temperature, no matter how pretty it is, is a waste of money and cigars.

Consider how you store your wine. You're protecting an investment. Your cigars are equally valuable and deserve a similar level of care.

The first step is to decide what size humidor you want. A good tip is to buy a humidor that's a little bigger than what you think you need. At the same time, you might want to investigate whether your local cigar retailer or cigar club has rental facilities which will let you store the bulk of your stock, so that you'll only need room for a few days' reserve at home or at work.

Just as if you were buying a new car, you'll want to look carefully at the construction and performance features of a humidor, as well as at its finish. If the seams aren't perfect, or if the corners aren't square, skip that humidor.

Pay particular attention to the rim and the lid, and how they fit together. The lid should shut tightly, but it should not "seal" completely; it should allow a minute amount of air to circulate in and out of the box. Any visible warping, however, will mean that too much air gets in and too much moisture gets out, even if there's a "lip" that fits inside the lid.

A heavy lid is generally an advantage. Many humidors, even those with locks, rely on the weight of the lid to keep them tightly shut. This, however, creates a challenge. A humidor

Danny
Marshall
humidor

should be designed to ensure balance, whether open or shut. If the lid opens too far, its weight can cause the humidor to flip up and fall over. If the lid doesn't open far enough to stay balanced in an upright position, it might come crashing back down on your fingers.

Locks aren't a bad idea. Consider the value –both emotional and financial—of the collection that you are going to keep in the humidor. Then consider the damage that could be done by prying fingers or even by malicious vandalism. You are likely to want a lock. Just be sure to have a duplicate key tucked away in a safe place. Nothing is more heartbreaking than to have to tamper with the perfectly-fitted and repeatedly-finished edges of a finely crafted humidor.

The first thing to notice on the inside of the box is the humidification device. Most humidification devices are relatively simple—little more than a sponge or a bottle that slowly emits moisture (consider an old-fashioned humidification device: apple cores!). The biggest variable in proper humidification,

Dunhill

after good construction, is not the type of humidification system you have, but whether or not you remember to add the needed water at regular intervals.

Look for a humidor lined with cedar. Cedar absorbs and re-emits moisture in a way that helps the various tobaccos blended into a fine cigar age and mature. If you are ambitious and handy enough to build your own humidor, be aware that you can't use just any cedar. Ask for Spanish cedar; the highly aromatic American cedar used to line closets and woolen chests would do disastrous things to the aroma of cigars. Some manufacturers today use mahogany or madroño—an evergreen native to the American West. These cousins of American cedar emit less odor and will not bleed resin.

The trays in humidors make it easy for you to organize, and occasionally rotate, your collection. The inside of a humidor experiences variations in humidity, despite the well or the slots which promote internal air circulation and reduce the likelihood that the base woods and the veneer will warp or separate. Within this microclimate, your driest cigars should be stored away from the humidification device so they re-attain proper hydration as slowly and evenly as possible.

Handles can be helpful on larger humidors, particularly if you will be moving the humidor around a room while offering cigars. If you are planning to put the humidor on a table or sideboard, a felt bottom will help protect both the humidor and the furniture.

Some humidors have magnets set into the underside of the lid, so you can store a cigar cutter there. This is good if it keeps you from misplacing an expensive cutter, and bad if it leads you to open the humidor more often or leave it open for longer periods of time. Before you get excited about a lid magnet, be sure to know the value of the cutter that it's supposed to hold. If you have scissors or a more expensive guillotine cutter, consider anchoring it to your humidor with an elegant chain, ensuring that the cutter will be available whenever you want to use it.

Finding a humidor with good construction and features isn't as hard as we've made it sound. Respectable humidor manufacturers are fanatical about quality control. Moreover,

Savinelli

reputable tobacconists will reject humidors with even minor functional defects.

Once you have decided on all of the basics and accessories concerning your humidor, allow yourself to be dazzled by the designs and finishes. Admire the gleaming rare-wood surfaces and catch the highlights dancing in a deep rich lacquer finish, or study the intricate marquetry picture. Marvel at some of the curved and sculptural shapes. You are buying a work of art. Be sure you love it: it's likely to be an important part of your home or office for many years to come.

Restoring Dried-Out Cigars

Most of the time, if you let cigars dry out, you have to write off your investment as tuition—often very expensive tuition. In some cases, cigars can be reconditioned through weeks in a good humidor. It's a tricky business, and one that should be left to someone with great patience and experience. If you insist on trying to do it yourself, proceed slowly. Over a period of several weeks, gradually move the cigars from the outside edges into the center of your humidor.

This is the only possible way to recondition a dried-out cigar. All of the other tales about how to restore dried-out cigars are merely interesting lore. Remember that a cigar has many layers of tobacco, and it is disastrous for the various layers to become moist or dry at different rates of speed. For example, if a cigar is placed in a hyper-moist environment and is then taken out of that environment, the outside dries and shrinks while the inside remains swollen, and the cigar splits open—not a pretty sight.

Here are some of the myths you may hear about restoring dried-out cigars. (Don't try them—EVER!):

- Put your cigars in the bathroom and run the shower until the hot water gives out
- Steam them in the upper rack of a dishwasher
- Sneak them into the steam room at the health club

Elie Bleu

How to Carry Cigars

When you take cigars with you on your travels, you need to protect them from physical damage, including drying. Travel humidors are an ideal solution. Many of them are compact enough to easily slip into your briefcase or the small bag you take on board aircraft—not that it's likely that you'll be allowed to smoke there.

When buying a travel humidor, first make sure that it will accommodate cigars of the size and shape you prefer. Then check it for durability. No matter how careful you are, your travel humidor will get jostled quite a bit. Make sure that it has a hinge that will stand up to a bit of abuse and repeated openings. (If you're a frequent international flyer, you'll find yourself constantly opening the case for U.S. customs inspectors who are hunting for Cuban cigars.) Also, make sure that the humid-ification unit will stay in place as you sprint for a taxi or jam your bag into an overhead compartment.

Even if you don't travel a lot, you may still want a travel humidor. They are extremely convenient for setting up a temporary depot of cigars in another part of your home. They are also perfect for keeping a few cigars humidified during the transition from a store's humidor to your own.

Sometimes, however, even a travel humidor is too big. Then you may want to rely on tubes and cigar cases. Tubos—cigars that come packed in tubes which help them stay properly humidified after they are taken out of a humidor—are a good one-at-a-time solution.

You can also purchase attractive silver or wooden tubes that will keep individual cigars properly moisturized for up to 72 hours. The drawback is that you will need several such tubes in order to carry a day's supply. On top of that, your tailor will hate them: they tend to be bulky and heavy and, when placed in a pocket, they ruin the "drape" of a garment.

Often, the answer is to carry an elegant leather cigar case

Diamond Crown

loaded with the cigars you hope to smoke that day and return any that you don't smoke to the humidor each evening.

If you always smoke the same kind of cigar, you can get a case that exactly fits your cigars—with "fingers" of the right diameter and with the ability to telescope if you favor long cigars. Fingered cases offer the best protection because they hold even a single cigar firmly in place.

If you smoke a varied selection, however, you will probably want to get an "open" case—one without separate dividers or molded fingers—which will accommodate a variety of sizes.

When you set out to buy a cigar case, wear the coat or jacket that has the smallest pockets of all the garments in your wardrobe. Make sure that the case fits and that you can live with the resulting bulge. Conversely, next time you have a suit, jacket, or coat fitted, be sure to bring your cigar case. A good tailor will be able to adapt the garment so you can carry the case without looking like you're packing a pistol.

Also, when buying a case, bring several cigars. (Or use the occasion as an excuse to buy a few.) The first test of any case is how well it fits your cigars. Load the case and see if you can slip the cigars in and out with reasonable ease. Close the case to make sure that it is not too short for your cigars.

You'll want the case to be lined so that your cigars won't take on a leathery taste and to prevent the tragedy of a fine cigar's wrapper snagging on rough, less-finished leather. The thickness of the leather is a matter of personal preference. The thicker the leather, the greater the protection. But thicker leather also adds weight and bulk.

Selecting the right cigar case can take a bit of time; there are more variables than you would think. Cigar cases are made with the same craftsmanship as fine footwear, and they come in almost as many different styles. Choose carefully. A fine cigar case is not only extremely functional, it is also an accessory which will distinguish you as a person of taste. And a wardrobe of cases is an appropriate investment in proper protection.

CHAPTER 7

THE GEOGRAPHY OF CIGAR
TOBACCO CULTIVATION

From Cuba to Connecticut

We have no idea how long people in the Americas enjoyed smoking tobacco before Christopher Columbus dropped anchor in Cuba's Bahía de Gibara harbor on October 29, 1492. But we do know that two explorers he sent inland saw Indians with "smoking heads." Columbus brought plant samples back to Europe. Tobacco smoking and sniffing wasn't instantly popular everywhere; in fact, some European rulers issued edicts against its use. But by the mid 1500s, only 50 years after its discovery by Europeans, tobacco had become a valuable commodity in global trade.

In the years between then and now, tobacco has been transplanted to many countries, and it continues to thrive in several of them today. Because tobacco is genetically stable—the seeds remain genetically pure from generation to generation—it would not be surprising if tobacco grown in new areas resulted in plants that were quite similar to their Central American forebears. In point of fact, however, even if plants from identical seeds are cultivated and fermented in exactly the same way, they will yield

Cultivating Connecticut shade wrapper leaf.

different-tasting tobacco if grown in two different places—just as single grape varieties as Cabernet Sauvignon or Chardonnay will yield strikingly varied wines, depending on where they're grown. Even subtle variations in soil and climate lead to noticeable differences in strength and flavor.

Cuba

Cuba has a long tradition as the source of the best cigar tobacco—to the extent that some time in the 19th century, premium cigars became known simply as Havanas (or Habanos). Cuban cigar tobacco is still acknowledged by many as setting the standard that the rest of the world follows. In general, Cuban tobacco is strong and full-bodied, with spicy and aromatic flavors. The leaves are renowned for their suppleness, an important attribute in the manufacturing of premium cigars.

Cuba's finest tobacco-growing area is the legendary Vuelta Abajo, part of the Pinar del Rio region in western Cuba. Other Cuban cigar-tobacco-growing areas are the Semi Vuelta area

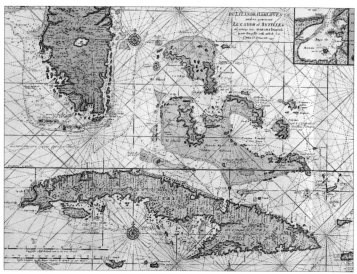

Cuba's rich tradition for cultivating great tobacco has long made its cigars the world's most celebrated.

(also in Pinar del Río), the Partido area in Havana province, and the Oriente and Remedios regions in the southeast.

Some smokers feel that the quality of Cuban tobacco has slipped in recent years, perhaps because that country's Communist regime has not offered sufficient incentives for fine tobacco production. Many aficionados, on the other hand, support their belief in the superiority of Cuban tobacco by citing the pride factor. The quality of the local tobacco is a matter of national pride in Cuba, much as the quality of local wines is in France. The workers in the tobacco-growing areas, and in the factories clustered in or near Havana, are proud of their expertise, which is passed on from generation to generation. Cigars are not just an export product for Cuba. Cubans are avid consumers of the cigars they produce.

Another factor behind the perception of declining quality may have to do with the explosion in counterfeit Cuban cigar brands, especially Cohiba and Montecristo. Even the most experienced smoker can at times be fooled into believing that a bogus cigar is real; when the counterfeit fails to enthrall, the smoker's opinion of the brand plummets.

The supremacy of Cuban tobacco is likely to remain one of the most passionately debated topics among cigar lovers. Someday soon, the relationship between the United States and Cuba may become less strained, and it will become easier for aficionados to obtain the supply of authentic Cuban cigars needed to form their own opinions on this issue.

The Dominican Republic

Some smokers maintain that the Dominican Republic's cigar tobacco, grown from Cuban seed and tended by experts trained in Cuba, has improved so greatly in recent decades that it now rivals Cuba's best. Although generally not quite as strong or spicy as Cuban tobacco, it tends to be quite full-flavored and contributes significantly to the creation of complex blends of filler tobacco.

Zones A, B, and C above are the Dominican Republic's prime tobacco growing areas. The Cibao Valley (Zones B and C) in particular is preeminent in tobacco quality and quantity.

The primary Dominican growing area is the Cibao River Valley, in the agricultural region near the city of Santiago in the northern half of the country. Santiago itself is home to a growing number of premium cigar factories.

Brazil

Brazilian tobacco leaves are distinctive indeed, as they are truly black in color after fermentation. They are grown mainly in the Cruz des Olmos region of Bahia Province, on the eastern Coast. Brazilian cigar tobacco tends to be full-bodied yet notably mild; it is often used to spice up a blend.

Ecuador

Ecuador is now producing a variety of tobaccos, including high-quality shade-grown and sun-grown wrapper, as well as filler. Growers here have successfully used seeds from both the Connecticut Valley and Sumatra. In each case, the Ecuadorian version seems milder and less robust in strength and flavor than the original. Ecuadorian wrappers have an appealing silky texture and their colors fall between that of the lighter Connecticut leaf and the darker Cameroon wrapper.

Honduras and Nicaragua

These Central American countries produce high-quality Cuban-seed and Connecticut-seed tobaccos—featuring shade-grown wrapper—that are full-bodied, with strong, spicy flavors and heady aromas. Tobacco grown in both Honduras and Nicaragua has suffered setbacks in recent years, however. Honduras has experienced periodic blue mold infestations. Nicaragua's production suffered during its prolonged civil war, much of which was fought in the tobacco region. With any luck, aficionados can look forward to an increase in the volume and quality of tobacco exported by these countries in the near future.

Mexico

The San Andres Valley is world-famous for a sun-grown variant of Sumatran-seed tobacco. Cigars manufactured in Mexico are usually made with 100-percent local tobacco. In addition, Mexican leaves are widely used as binder and filler in cigars manufactured in other countries.

Mexican wrapper leaves are often used as maduro wrappers, because they stand up well to the cooking and sweating process that creates the darker leaf colors.

United States

The Connecticut River Valley, north of Hartford, Connecticut, produces "Connecticut Shade," some of the finest wrapper-leaf tobacco in the world. This fine brown to brownish-yellow leaf, noted for its elasticity, creates a mild- to medium-bodied smoke, and is widely used for premium cigars.

Another variety grown in this valley is "Connecticut Broadleaf." Its heavier, dark (almost black), heavily veined leaf is used on maduro cigars.

A glance at the world's most productive cigar tobacco growing regions.

Cameroon / Central African Republic

In recent years, bad weather and management changes have kept this area of West Africa from fulfilling its potential to produce high-quality wrapper leaf. The Cameroon leaf originated from Sumatran seeds imported from Indonesia. It is prized for its neutral characteristics, which make it an ideal wrapper for

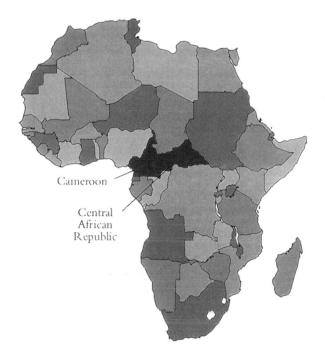

Cameroon

Central
African
Republic

full-flavored filler tobaccos. Cameroon wrappers are generally greenish-brown to dark brown. Aficionados recognize Cameroon by its distinct grain, called tooth.

Indonesia

The tobacco that comes from the series of islands that make up Indonesia may be referred to as Java or Sumatra. Sumatran wrapper leaves are often dark brown and have neutral flavors. The majority of the wrapper grown here is used in the manufacture of small cigars.

Philippines

A mild cigar tobacco is grown in the Philippines. The hybrid strain produced here is very aromatic.

CHAPTER 8

THE MAKING OF
PREMIUM CIGARS

The Art of the Torcedor

The making of a premium, hand-rolled cigar is a complicated process. In some factories, a leaf may be touched by human hands up to 40 times before the cigar is finally completed. The dedication of the tobacco growers, harvesters, fermenters, and rollers is something that you should consider in depth before lighting up. Your experience will be more rewarding when you understand that your cigar is the work of dedicated craftsmanship.

Growing the Tobacco

Cigar tobacco reaches the factory after three periods of approximately six weeks each (known as the "magic sixes"): six weeks to germinate seeds before transplanting them into a field; six weeks for the tobacco plant to grow to maturity; six weeks for a complete harvest. The length of any of these periods can vary with the weather, the quality of the crop, and the particular end product that the leaf will be used to make.

Fermenting the Tobacco

After the tobacco is harvested, it goes through a series of fermentation processes. In the initial fermentation stage, workers pile slightly moistened tobacco into huge bales or stacks, called bulks. As the tobacco ferments, or "sweats," temperatures inside the bulks reach as high as 140°F. Workers assure even fermentation by breaking down the bulks, re-moistening and

A fresh crop of Connecticut shade.

then rebuilding them. Some tobacco may be "turned" up to four times before this stage of fermentation is completed. During this stage, the tobacco releases ammonia, and its overall nicotine content is reduced.

Workers then wrap the fermented tobacco in bales, usually surrounded by burlap, to age. Standard aging time is 18 months to two years, although some manufacturers keep inventories of tobacco as old as 10 years. Before workers turn over the tobacco to the hand-rollers, they case it, or slightly dampen it again, to make it supple and easy to work with.

Hand-Crafting the Cigar

A cigar blend is created by a master blender, someone who combines tobaccos of varying tastes and strengths to create a particular taste in a balanced, harmonious smoke. Depending on its ring gauge, a cigar will contain a blend of between two and four different tobaccos. Each type of tobacco leaf is placed in different boxes on the desk of a *torcedor*—a professional cigar roller. The rollers are then given the formula for the cigars they are making.

The rollers take the leaves and press them gently together in their hands. Then they place the leaves on a binder leaf—a flat, somewhat elastic leaf of tobacco. The tobacco is rolled together into a bunch, cut to the appropriate length and placed in the bottom half of a wooden mold. After the upper half of the mold is attached, the entire box is placed in a screw press (see photo, pg. 116). The press operator will usually break down the press once, turn the bunch inside the mold, and then rebox and press the bunch again, for a total pressing time of about an hour.

The wooden molds are then returned to the rolling tables. The roller removes the bunch and completes the cigar with a wrapper leaf—a supple and visually beautiful leaf that has been

A torcedor, or cigar roller, works his craft.

119

cut in half. Keeping constant pressure on the bunch and the wrapper, the cigar maker rolls the leaf around the bunch and applies a bit of vegetable glue to bond the wrapper leaf together at the head so the cigar won't unravel.

A skilled artisan can make from 75 to 150 cigars a day, depending on the size and shape of the cigar and the manufacturing process. When rollers work on a team, the production rate increases to 200–400 cigars a day.

Supervisors inspect each cigar by hand. They feel it for weight and for any hard spots, which could indicate a plug, or soft spots, which can cause an uneven burn. They reject defective cigars. Then, in most factories, workers weigh the cigars in bunches of 50. Bunches produced by skilled rollers will vary by less than one gram. Bunches with significant weight variations

After tobacco leaves are harvested, and before they begin to ferment, they are hung to dry in large wooden barns called casas de tabaco.

may be returned to the roller to be reworked.

The construction of a cigar is crucial. Even the best tobaccos will taste bad if they are in a cigar that burns too quickly or too slowly.

Aging the Cigar

The next stop for cigars is the aging room. Most factories age their cigars at least 21 days, and some leave them in the aging room for anywhere from 90 to 180 days. This allows the different cigar tobaccos to "marry" and create a more balanced smoke. After aging, the cigars are selected for each box, checked for fine gradations in leaf color, and finally packed in boxes for shipping.

CHAPTER 9
CIGAR COLORS, SHAPES, AND SIZES
There's Something for Everyone

Cigar wrappers come in a palette of colors that resemble human skin tones. Just as scientists describe the rainbow in seven basic colors, aficionados use seven basic color descriptions for wrappers, although there are many subtle shades among these basic colors. Some cigar merchants describe cigars in many more than seven hues. The easiest way to understand this color scale is to remember that, just as the state of Colorado is in the middle of the United States (more or less), the color "Colorado" is in the middle of the range of wrapper colors.

The variation in wrapper color is a result of how the wrapper leaf is processed, as well as the color variations among different types of tobacco and the amount of sunlight a leaf is exposed to (which in turn depends on how high up on the plant the leaf was located).

From light to dark, the seven commonly used wrapper color descriptions are:

Double Claro, also called *Candela*—A light green to yellow shade achieved by a heat-assisted quick-drying process that retains the chlorophyll content of wrapper leaves. At one time, Americans showed a preference for these slightly sweet-tasting wrappers, and Europeans looked down on them for it. Since then, both American and European tastes have broadened.

Claro—A light tan color; usually achieved by growing under shade tents, picking the leaves before they mature, and quickly air-drying them. Claro wrappers are relatively neutral in flavor and let the flavors of the "bunch"—the tobacco inside the cigar—shine through on a consistent basis.

Colorado Claro or Natural—Light brown; most often sun-grown.

Colorado—A medium-brown to brownish-red shade of wrapper leaf. Usually shade-grown and characterized by rich flavor and subtle aroma.

Colorado Maduro—Darker than colorado, lighter than maduro.

Maduro—A shade of wrapper varying from a very dark reddish-brown to almost black. The word means "ripe" in Spanish, a reference to the longer process needed to produce this

Double Claro *Claro* *Colorado Claro or Natural* *Colorado*

kind of wrapper: the leaves are either "cooked" in a pressure chamber or fermented for a longer period of time in hotter-than-normal conditions. Maduro wrappers impart a distinct character to a cigar: they taste as different as they look. They generally have a mild aroma, but a strong, slightly sweet flavor.

Oscuro—This darker-than-maduro shade is produced by leaving the wrapper leaves on the plant the longest; by using only the leaves from the very top of the tobacco plant, which have had the most sun; and by fermenting, or "sweating," them the longest. It's sometimes called "black" or "negro." Oscuro wrappers are often Brazilian or Mexican in origin.

Colorado   *Maduro*   *Oscuro*
Maduro

Shapes and Sizes

Traditional cigar shapes, or formats, vary greatly in size from brand to brand, so it's important to describe cigars by their dimensions—length and diameter—as well as by their shape. In the U.S., U.K., and Cuba, length is measured in inches and diameter is designated in ring gauge—a measurement divided into 64ths of an inch. A cigar with a ring gauge of 42, for example, has a diameter of 42/64ths of an inch. (In other countries, length is given in centimeters, and diameter in millimeters.) Fine cigars are not weighed, except for quality-control purposes in the factory.

Despite certain myths, there is no correspondence between the size of a cigar and its strength. Large cigars made with mild tobaccos are mellow, while small cigars made with strong-flavored tobaccos are powerful. Additionally, there is no consistency from brand to brand: one company's lonsdale is likely to taste very different from another's.

Parejos: straight-sided cigars

Straight-sided cigars are the most common shape, but there are many subtle differences among them.

Coronas

Coronas have traditionally been the benchmark against which all other cigar formats are measured. They generally have an open "foot" for lighting and a closed, rounded "head" which you cut before smoking.

Petit Corona. This short corona is usually only 4½ inches, with a ring gauge of 40 to 42.

Corona. The traditional dimensions are 5½ to 6 inches with a ring gauge of 42 to 44.

Churchill. A large corona format. The traditional dimensions are 7 inches by a 48 ring gauge.

Robusto. A short Churchill format that is growing in popularity. The traditional size is 5 to 5½ inches by a stocky 50 ring gauge.

Corona Gorda. This long robusto format could be called a robusto extra, although its popularity preceded that of robustos. The traditional measurements are 5⅝ inches by a 46 ring gauge.

Double Corona. The standard dimensions are 7½ to 8 inches by a 49 to 52 ring gauge.

Panatela

Shaped like a longer, thinner corona, panatelas were more popular in years past than they are today. This format varies in length from 5 to 7½ inches and has a ring gauge of 34 to 38.

Lonsdale

A lonsdale is generally thicker than a panatela, but longer than a corona. The classic size is 6¾ inches by a 42 to 44 ring gauge.

Figurados: unusually shaped cigars

Although most cigars are straight-sided cylinders with one rounded end, there are a number of traditional cigar formats with more novel shapes—the figurados. Different manufacturers have interpreted these names differently, so you might, for example, find a cigar that fits the description below of a "pyramid," but is called a "belicoso." There is no perfect consensus, but generally here's what the figurados look like:

Pyramid

A sharply tapered- and closed-headed cigar with a wider open foot. These cigars measure between 6 and 7 inches long with a ring gauge of around 40 at the head that widens to 52 to 54 at the foot.

Belicoso

Traditionally, a belicoso was a short pyramid, 5 or 5½ inches in length with a shorter, more rounded taper at the head and a ring gauge generally of 50 or less. Today, belicosos are frequently coronas or corona gordas with a tapered head.

Torpedo

A torpedo has a closed foot, a pointed head, and a bulge in the middle.

Perfecto

Like a torpedo, the perfecto has a closed foot and a bulge in the middle. The difference is that the head is rounded rather than pointed. Perfectos can vary greatly in length (three sizes are shown on page 131), from 4½ to 9 inches, and can have a ring gauge between 38 and 48.

Culebra

This exotic shape, made up of three panatelas braided together and banded as one cigar, makes it clear why cigars have sometimes been called "ropes." The three parts are unbraided and smoked separately. They are usually 5 to 6 inches in length, most often with a 38 ring gauge. Culebras are relatively rare these days. If you acquire one, you might consider finding two other cigar aficionados and turning the smoking of your culebra into an occasion.

Diademas

A big cigar—8 inches or longer. The head is closed and tapered, with a ring gauge of 40. The foot can be open, or closed like a perfecto, and is a healthy 52 ring gauge, or larger.

Petit
Corona

Corona

Robusto

Corona
Gorda

Churchill

Double
Corona

Panatela

Lonsdale

Pyramid

Belicoso

Torpedo

*Cuban
Perfecto*

Perfecto

Perfecto

Culebra

Diademas

131

CHAPTER 10

CIGARS AND SPIRITS

A Fruitful Marriage

A true aficionado does not limit his or her pursuit of happiness but develops familiarity with a wide range of beverages to enhance the pleasure of a premium cigar. Wine is the first one that comes to mind. There is a growing number of people who believe that no meal is complete unless it is accompanied by a fine wine and a premium cigar. You probably already know a little about wines and champagne. If not, there are plenty of people eager to educate you. You probably also have picked up some knowledge about better beers and ales, and about coffee.

In addition, however, there are a few other beverages that are natural partners for cigars.

Cognacs and Brandies

What do Cognacs and brandies have to do with fine cigars? Nothing —and everything. Certainly, there are cigar aficionados who don't indulge in, or even enjoy, Cognacs and brandies. There are even a good many teetotaling cigar enthusiasts. But for many more, fine cigars are delicately linked to these fine spirits. They appeal to the same mature, trained palates. While you are learning to appreciate cigars, you may want to explore these choice libations as well.

Brandies inspire passionate discussion among connoisseurs. Loyal patrons have been known to claim that brandy, a product distilled from grapes, is to wine what cigars are to cigarettes. Distillers in the Cognac and Armagnac regions of France claim a superiority for their regional products similar to the rank that Cuba claims for its cigars. Other enthusiasts make a strong case

Cognac is one of the finest complements to a premium cigar.

for Spanish and American brandies. Still others argue for the merits of other grape-based spirits such as grappa or marc.

In due time, you'll want to try all these options and evaluate each particular potion for yourself. But, since you are probably smoking superior cigars, you might as well start at the top, with Cognac, which is created by a unique double distillation process.

Cognac Regions

To be called Cognac, a spirit must come from a small, clearly-defined region surrounding the town of Cognac in France. The people of Cognac are quite serious about their traditions, skills, and exclusivity. In Cognac, as in real estate, location is of utmost importance.

The town of Cognac is surrounded by a circle of six growing areas which produce the grapes—mostly of the Ugni Blanc variety—used to make Cognac. Within that circle is an area called Grande Champagne, which is said to produce the very best Cognacs. Another Cognac-producing area is called Petit Champagne which is actually larger than the Grande Champagne (as if associating the name "Champagne" with Cognac weren't confusing enough). The other four areas are: Borderies, Fins Bois, Bons Bois, and Bois Communs (or Ordinaires).

Each of these areas produces grapes with a distinct flavor. Master Cognac blenders often create great Cognacs by using grapes grown by a variety of sources in all six areas. This blending of grapes is quite similar to the blending of tobaccos in the filler of a premium cigar. A designation of "Fine Champagne" Cognac means that 50 percent of its grapes came from the Grande Champagne area. If all the grapes came from either the Grande Champagne or the Petite Champagne region, this may be indicated on the bottle's label. Such variations make Cognac tasting complex, fascinating, and rewarding.

Cognac Age Designations

Much of Cognac's distinct flavor develops while it is aging in French oak barrels. The longer a Cognac is aged, the better, and more expensive, it will be. If a Cognac bottle is marked "V.S.," its contents were aged in the barrel for less than four and a half years. "V.S.O.P." Cognac has been aged for more than four and a half years, while "X.O." means that a Cognac has been aged for more than six and a half years. X.O. Cognac is also called "Napoleon."

As special and precious as an X.O. Cognac is, there are

A bartender at the Four Seasons restaurant in New York takes a break; the Four Seasons bar is a popular place to enjoy a cocktail and a cigar.

some Cognacs that are produced with even more care. Many brands produce extra special Cognacs that are aged for far longer than six and a half years, and sometimes for as many as 70 years. Courvoisier Initiale Extra, Hennessy Paradis, Hine Triomphe, Martell Extra, and Remy Martin Louis XIII are all extraordinary examples of Cognac at its best.

Armagnac

Once you've learned to appreciate Cognac, you should try Armagnac for contrast. It is only distilled once and, although also barrel-aged, it lacks Cognac's extraordinary smoothness. However, the single distillation lets it retain more of the flavor of the grapes from which it's made. Like wine, Armagnac is frequently bottled in specific years, or vintages. Ordering Armagnac in a French restaurant, or in a bar in France, indicates to many that you are a true connoisseur.

Grappa and Marc

If you find you have—or, more likely, develop—a taste for the somewhat rougher, more powerful flavor of Armagnac, you may want to sample two other forms of liquid lightning: grappa and marc. These grape-based spirits, which are rarely tempered by significant barrel-aging, deliver a powerful kick. They can stand up to even the strongest cigars.

For years, Italians have delighted in introducing travelers to the delights of their deceptively clear local grappas. (If you find yourself in a grappa drinking contest with a little old man or woman in a small town in Italy, you should understand two things: 1) you are going to lose, and 2) you will feel horrible the next day.) Now, Americans are catching on, and American vineyards are producing grappas, too. The competition seems to be elevating the state of the art. Single-grape variety grappas with more clearly distinct flavors are becoming available.

After the grapes are crushed to make fine wines, wine-makers use the leftover material, the "must," to make a treat for themselves: marc. Marc is still considered a secondary product and is often hard to find—so don't pass up any opportunity you have to try it.

Spanish and American Brandy

The Spanish have a distinct brandy tradition. Spanish brandy is dark and rich, and is often made from wine grapes from the Valdepenas region. It rewards those who sip it with a sweet and fragrant flavor. People who like to dip cigars in brandy often use Spanish brandy. If you do this, be prepared to face ridicule from conservatives who consider this practice an insult to both the cigar and the brandy.

Once largely the province of cooks (and winos looking for a high-proof product), American brandies have come into their own in recent years. Typical California brandies are light and mellow, with a pronounced grapey flavor, and range from quite dry to quite sweet. Some smaller "boutique" producers are now using the more traditional pot stills, which allow them to make brandies with a distinctive individual character. It is probable that American brandies will soon reach the levels of excellence already established for American wines.

Port

The ritual of retiring to the drawing room for Port and cigars has changed a bit since the 1800s. In the old days, only men were allowed to engage in these pleasures; women weren't invited into the room for any reason. The combination of Port and a fine cigar is still the quintessential cap to a wonderful meal. These days, few would even *think* to shut the ladies out.

Apropros to a beverage most often served after dinner, Port has a dessert-like richness and sweetness. While it takes years for most people to develop an appreciation for some spirits, Port is immediately attractive and tasty to the majority. Of course, you can also spend years learning to appreciate the subtleties of Port, too.

Port is a fortified wine, a wine to which brandy has been added to boost its alcohol content to about 20 percent. It is made from grapes grown in vineyards called "quintas" in Portugal's Upper Douro Valley, and is blended in and shipped from the coastal town of Oporto—hence its name.

If Port is from Portugal, why do we associate it with England? In fact, it was the British who developed not only the Port trade, but Port itself as we know it today. In 1703, in the midst of a war with France (Britain's main wine source), Queen Anne's ambassador signed a commercial treaty giving Portuguese wine preferential tax treatment. Though cheap, the harsh natural wines were not immediately popular in England. But a group of enterprising British wine merchants in Oporto soon discovered that if brandy were added to the wine before all the sugar had fermented into alcohol, not only would the wine survive its long sea voyage better, but its smoother character would appeal more to English tastes.

You've probably heard of "Vintage Port." Vintage, in this

A glass of port and a fine cigar are the quintessential cap to a wonderful meal.

case, does not mean old. It means that the Port is from one of the years that the producer or shipper has declared to be a superior, or "vintage," year. Once a vintage is declared, the port is aged in wooden casks for two years before it is bottled.

There isn't always agreement among the many suppliers as to whether a given year is "vintage," but generally, vintage port will be better than non-vintage port. The main thing you need to know about vintage years is that great Ports mature over many years. Thirty-, forty-, or even fifty-year-old Ports can be at their peak.

Good-quality Ports from a non-vintage year can become something called "late-bottled vintage" (LBV) Ports. These are products of a single harvest that are aged in wood for four to six years (i.e., twice as long as true Vintage Ports), and are ready to drink when purchased. They are meant to approximate the character of Vintage Ports (though without the same depth of flavor), at less expense and without the inconvenience to the consumer of long cellaring.

The least expensive ports of all are called Ruby Ports. These are young, blended wines that retain their bright red color and sweet, fruity character. They spend just long enough in a barrel (two to three years) to be potable when released.

Finally, there is Tawny Port. It too is made by blending non-vintage fortified wines and wood-aging the blend, but in this case the aging period may be as long as 10, 20, or even 30 years. (The age designations on a bottle of Tawny, such as "20-year-old," refer to the average age of the wines in the blend; some of the ingredients may be younger.) The long period in wood leads to the wine's faded color and refined, nutty flavor. Some Tawnies are ordinary in quality, but others—blended and aged with supreme care by their makers—are among the greatest of all Ports.

The leading Port houses—producing the finest of Ports—include Cockburn, Croft, Dow, Fonseca, Graham, Quinta do Noval, Taylor Fladgate, and Warre.

Once you've learned to enjoy Port, you'll want to try combining specific Ports with specific cigars. The flavors complement and enhance each other so well, it's no wonder they are so often enjoyed together.

Scotch Whisky and Irish Whiskey

The growing appreciation of premium cigars and Scotch and Irish whiskeys have been some of the most powerful taste trends in recent years. It's a logical progression. Fermented and aged malted barley yields flavors of a richness and complexity similar to the flavors created by fermenting choice cigar tobaccos. And both Scotch and cigars are available in countless, subtle variations which reward and intrigue aficionados.

Traditionally, most Americans have been familiar with Scotches made from a blend of fine malt spirits and neutral grain spirits. In recent years, the popularity of single malt Scotch whiskies has taken off. A "single malt" is, as the name implies, a non-blended Scotch made with spirits from a single distillery which processes the natural products grown in its immediate vicinity.

Each single malt has a distinct taste which reflects the characteristics of the local soil and climate and which proves the value of its closely-guarded distilling processes. Single malt distillers proudly advertise how long they age their potent potables. They may even tell whether they use old Sherry or Bourbon barrels for aging their precious concoction. (If that information is not on the label, consider this: Sherry casks add a certain sweetness to aged Scotch whisky that the Bourbon casks don't.) But it is highly unlikely that they will disclose their exact recipe.

Irish whiskeys do not have the devoted following that Scotch whiskies have gained, but they do have, and have always had, a minority of loyal fans. Because they tend to be triple-distilled, Irish whiskeys are generally more neutral in flavor than the earthier Scotch whiskies.

Scotches are hardly delicate in flavor, and they can generally stand up to soda and ice. But the subtlety and complexity of a fine Scotch can best be appreciated when it is served "neat," without water, mixers, or ice. Scotch-based cocktails such as the Rusty Nail (Scotch and Drambuie) and the Rob Roy (Scotch

A fine single malt whisky will double the pleasure of a premium cigar.

141

and sweet vermouth) have faded in popularity as people have started drinking and appreciating better Scotches straight up.

Fine whiskeys, like premium cigars, are an acquired taste—and a taste well worth acquiring. Don't be surprised if, in a short while, you can discern whether the amber fluid in your glass comes from Speyside, Lowlands, Highlands, Campbeltown, or Islay.

Rum

A few years ago, rum was considered by many to be merely an inexpensive spirit that fueled tropical drinks. But remember, just a few years ago many thought that a good cigar was one that came with a plastic tip on it. Just as aficionados in the U.S. have learned the art of cigar appreciation, they are learning to savor the flavor and smoothness of dark, aged rums. (Rum, by the way, was first distilled at least 3,000 years ago in Asia and made its way to North Africa before becoming a Caribbean commodity.)

Elementary-school history classes often included lessons about "the triangle trade," a commercial pattern that involved shipping molasses from the Caribbean islands to the American colonies. In case your history teacher didn't explain it fully, the reason there was such a demand for molasses (made from sugar cane) is because it's the material that's needed to process rum.

There is greater variety in the distillation of rums than there is in the creation of most other spirits. The cleaner, more neutral rums are often the product of modern column stills. Some other rums are the result of slow, natural fermentation processes that take over a week. Some controlled fermentation processes are accelerated through the use of yeasts.

The resulting distillate is then aged in white oak Bourbon barrels. The inside of these barrels is charred, and the reactions between the charred surfaces and the rum add flavor and color. The longer a rum is aged, the smoother it tends to become. United States law requires that the age printed on a bottle of rum should be the age of the youngest rum used in the blend.

If you are drinking a "five-year-old" rum, it's quite possible that a good portion of it is twice that old.

In addition to spotting the age on a bottle, it's a good idea to check the proof. Some rums are more powerful than others and may sneak up on you if you aren't aware that they are packing extra proof.

Because rum is made according to different traditions on different islands, it's worth sampling rums from as many different places as possible. Puerto Ricans are often proud of their light rums, while Barbados and the Virgin Islands argue that rum should have a bit more "body," as theirs do. Bermuda, Guatemala, and Jamaica proudly proffer even darker rums.

You should form your own opinion on this international issue. Never leave a Caribbean island before you have sampled their local rum; and make sure to take advantage of the duty-free prices on your return trip, so you can continue the holiday experience at home.

Despite their differences, almost every one of these countries concurs on two matters: First, that rum has been underrated, and second, that rum and cigars are perfect companions. As proof of this, they are likely to cite the fact that many professional cigar tasters (now there's an enviable job!) cleanse their palates between cigars with a swirl of rum, rather than water. They say the rum enhances the cigars' flavor.

Tequila

Tequila plays the same role in Mexico that rum plays in the Caribbean and wine plays in France. It is the center of a proud agricultural and manufacturing tradition, and the "locals" pity the rest of the world for not having yet learned all the wonders of their unique, magical potion.

Like rum, tequila first became known in the United States as a base for mixed drinks and has only lately been appreciated for its own flavor.

Tequila is made from the blue agave plant (known to

botanists as *agave Tequilana Weber*). Its flavor changes as it ages. An unaged tequila is likely to have more flavor, while an aged—reposado or añejo—tequila will be smoother.

To get an idea of just how sublime tequila can be, find a bar or restaurant that offers a dozen or more tequilas and order a 100-percent blue agave tequila in a snifter. Then treat it like a fine wine or Cognac, swirling and sipping it so you get the full impact of its bouquet, flavor, and finish.

For the record, you won't find a worm in a tequila bottle. The legendary worm only swims in the bottle of certain brands of mescal, a harsher relative of tequila.

Kentucky Bourbon and Other American Whiskeys

The United States has also made important contributions to the world of spirits: Kentucky Bourbon and other American whiskeys.

If you believe the legend, Bourbon was accidentally invented after fire struck Elijah Craig's warehouse and charred some of the barrels he used to ship his potent "white lightning." Craig determined that the barrels were watertight and filled them despite the charring. He may have been prepared for complaints, but all he got were compliments and requests for more. On the way to the market in New Orleans, his distilled spirits had interacted with the burned barrels, taking on a new amber color and a superior, mellower flavor.

Bourbon is no longer created by accident; there are strict regulations that must be met in order to earn the name. To be called "Bourbon," a spirit must be from Kentucky. It must be made from at least 51 percent corn. In fact, most distillers use a higher percentage of corn, up to 75 percent, with wheat or other grains making up the balance of the fermentation mash. And while Elijah Craig's first batch of Bourbon was freshly distilled, today's Bourbons must be aged for at least two years in charred white-oak barrels.

Bourbons, and quality American whiskeys from states other than Kentucky, are experiencing a Renaissance similar to the one enjoyed by better beers and single-malt Scotches. The number of brands is proliferating as master artisans create small-batch and single-barrel products. Consumers are starting to appreciate the fine differences between Kentucky Bourbon and the sweeter, smokier, charcoal filtered spirits often made in neighboring states, such as Tennessee.

More established Bourbons, made by blending the contents of many different barrels, are still being mixed into Whiskey Sours and Mint Juleps, but the premium boutique brands—including one named after our old friend Elijah Craig—are being treated like fine wines. They are sipped, tasted, rated, and compared in bars, restaurants, and homes across the country. For the most part, they are served neat, although there are some who say that a bit of water or an ice cube or two releases more of a Bourbon's flavors.

When you start sampling Bourbons to find your favorites, watch out for those labeled "cask strength." They are bottled without being cut with water, so they can range up to 126 proof.

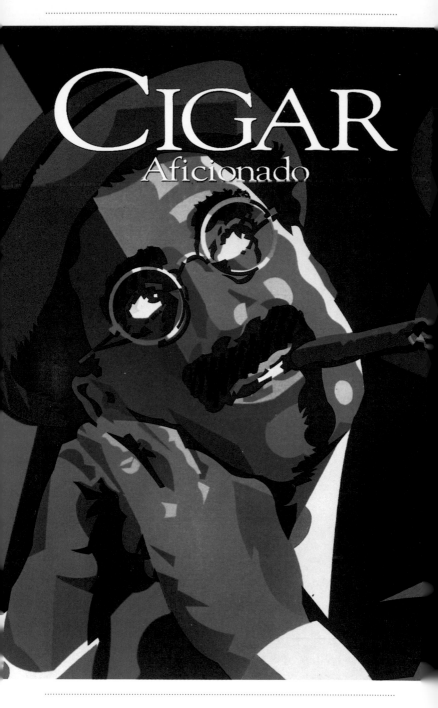

CHAPTER 11

A CENTURY OF CIGARS

From King Edward VII to
Cigar Aficionado *Magazine*

I f you look at pictures from the turn of the century, from anywhere in the Western world, you'll notice that most of the men are wearing hats—and holding cigars. The cigar has always been a mark of accomplishment and leadership. Kings, presidents, generals, and gentlemen all smoked, and so did a fair number of women. Politicians, of course, always smoked cigars: that's how the back rooms—where deals were made—got to be "smoke-filled" in the first place. It is estimated that, in 1900, four out of every five U.S. men smoked cigars.

But cigar smoking always had its opponents. Queen Victoria of England was known for her vehement disapproval of tobacco in any form. So it was no surprise that a distinct sigh of relief accompanied her son Edward's announcement at Buckingham Palace- -upon ascending to the throne at age 61 in 1901—"Gentlemen, you may proceed to smoke."

In the U.S., many of the reactionary forces which fought "demon rum" and brought about Prohibition in the U.S. in 1919 also fought tobacco. This was not a pleasure-loving bunch. They fiercely battled to enforce their standards of hygiene, morals, diet, and clothing over the rest of the country. Also, the social perception was spread that smoking was "unladylike."

Still, on the whole, the 1920s were not only "roaring," they were also "smoking." When Vice President Thomas Riley Marshall said, "What this country really needs is a good five-cent cigar" while presiding over the U. S. Senate in 1920, everyone understood that he hoped more people could share the pleasure.

Fidel Castro seized control of Cuba in 1959.

Marshall eventually got his wish—and then some. Cigarettes, once thought to be a feminine affectation compared to cigars, got a big boost from World War I. Cigarettes were more convenient and readily available to the average soldier, as they could be mass-manufactured and packed with the rations.

In fear of losing market share, cigar manufacturers moved quickly to adopt mechanization, prices fell dramatically, and by the Great Depression, the cigar had become a working man's smoke.

Meanwhile, particularly in Europe, the tradition of providing premium, hand-rolled Havana cigars to the well-to-do continued. In 1907, Alfred Dunhill opened a store in London devoted to fine tobacco products; Rudyard Kipling and Winston Churchill were among his clients. Dunhill was a master of marketing and advertising and was among the first to recognize the importance of humidifying and aging cigars before they were sold to his privileged customers. Alfred Dunhill opened his first store in New York City in 1921.

World War II brought further upheavals to the cigar world. Unable to get Havanas during the war years, British smokers turned to premium cigars from the crown colony of Jamaica, thus giving impetus to the diffusion of cigar manufacturing throughout the Caribbean. (The war also gave an inadvertent boost to the career of Zino Davidoff, along with Dunhill one of the 20th century's legendary cigar retailers. The Davidoff family, emigrants from Kiev, opened their first tobacco shop in Geneva in 1929. In the early 1940s, Zino acquired a large stock of Havanas that had belonged to the Vichy French government and was thenceforth able to supply his European customers with cigars they could get nowhere else.)

In 1900, four out of five U.S. men smoked cigars.

After World War II Cuban cigars became newly popular in the United States, where smokers had previously favored the domestic, machine-made product. Both true Havanas and so-called "clear Havanas"—cigars made in the U.S. (usually Tampa) from imported Cuban bulk tobacco— were purchased in large numbers. But alas, Americans' love affair with Havanas was to be short-lived.

In 1959, Cuba—where much of the world's premium cigar-making expertise was concentrated—underwent Fidel Castro's Communist revolution. Relations between the U.S. and Cuba deteriorated and, in February 1962, President John F. Kennedy authorized a full trade embargo against the island

President John F. Kennedy's 1962 trade embargo against Cuba is still in effect.

nation (an embargo that has remained in effect up until the time of this publication).

In 1964, a U.S. Surgeon General's report—known as the Terry Report—labeled tobacco as a contributing factor in cancer, heart disease, and other ailments. The report carefully distinguished between cigarette smoke (which is inhaled) and cigar smoke, which is not inhaled and is therefore less of a medical risk.

Perhaps because of this relatively clean bill of health, cigars remained popular in the U.S. for a while; consumption peaked in the early 1970s, when around 11 million cigars of all types were smoked annually. But at this point the tide began to turn. Some smokers felt that the (non-Cuban) cigars they could now get were not worth smoking. Others were discouraged by a wave of anti-smoking sentiment that began to sweep through the nation.

Anti-smoking lobbies developed throughout the U.S.— and to a lesser extent, Europe—and were successful in limiting smoking through legislation. Local laws were created to ban smoking in public buildings. Smoking was prohibited on all domestic airline flights in the U.S.

The anti-smoking forces may have felt they had won the day. But they underestimated the determination and commitment of the U.S. cigar culture. In certain families, elders continued to tell the children family tales of respected cigar-smoking ancestors. Also, the demands of international business brought Americans in contact with the rest of the world, where Cuban products were still allowed. Smokers kept smoking cigars, including the many Cuban cigars that somehow made it into the U.S. each year despite the trade embargo.

This political turmoil resulted in confusion among cigar smokers when a number of Cuba's master cigar-makers fled to other shores. These refugee Cuban cigar makers continued to make cigars under the same brand names they had used in Cuba. Meanwhile, the businesses they had left behind were taken over (nationalized) by Castro loyalists who also continued to use the same popular brand names. A Punch, for example, could either come from Cuba or Honduras. A Partagas may have been rolled in the Dominican Republic or in Cuba. And the only way to know if a Cohiba, Montecristo, El Rey del Mundo, Romeo y Julieta, La Gloria Cubana, Fonseca, or H. Upmann is Cuban or not—until you are enough of an aficionado to recognize Cuban wrapper leaf—is to look for a small Habano or Havana on the band.

The confusion was, however, a small price to pay for the creation of new resources for quality cigars. Cigar makers from outside of Cuba noticed the gap in the U. S. market created by the Cuban embargo and soon took to filling it. Just as the U.S. was ready to appreciate them, an abundance of new premium cigars from a host of countries was made available. The stage was set for a cigar renaissance —all that was needed was a catalyst.

Then, in 1992, *Cigar Aficionado* magazine was born. Would-be smokers turned to it for education; long-time cigar smokers welcomed it as a forum to unite like-minded aficionados. A sizable, affluent segment of the population started lighting up—in public! "Cigar dinners" sprang up across the country as smokers gratefully combined the satisfaction of fine cuisine, the joys of camaraderie, and the exquisite pleasures of cigars.

As the U.S. approaches the twenty-first century, it has accepted a much more open attitude toward cigars than it has held in a long time. Certainly, there are still plenty of vociferous opponents, but the cigar movement is too strong to be stopped. A few politicians, who have been cigar aficionados all along, are now allowing pictures to be taken of them smoking. Some of the country's best athletes are admitting they smoke cigars, and it clearly hasn't hurt their performances—or their images!

Hollywood has never deserted the cause. Producers have always favored fine cigars, and the current generation of stars is studded with cigar aficionados: Arnold Schwarzenegger, Tom Selleck, Bruce Willis, Sylvester Stallone, Bill Cosby, Jack Nicholson, Jim Belushi, Danny DeVito, and Harvey Keitel have all brandished their favorite sticks for the paparazzi.

What's more, many women have joined the ranks of cigar enthusiasts. It has become more difficult for cigar critics to turn cigar smoking into a men-versus-women issue now that Madonna, Linda Evangelista, Sharon Stone, Drew Barrymore, Whoopi Goldberg, Lauren Hutton, Demi Moore, and a legion of other women are regularly seen enjoying their cigars.

Cuban cigars have been banned in the U. S. since 1962, but there are signs that the diplomatic freeze may finally be thawing. With the Cold War over, it's increasingly difficult for U. S. politicians to continue to portray Cuba as a legitimate enemy and threat. If relationships are normalized between these countries, American aficionados will get to conduct their own taste tests to see if—as some people claim—other islands have surpassed Cuba in their ability to produce premium cigars of the finest quality.

The U.S. may never top the cigar consumption level it reached in the early 1970s, and that's just fine. While Americans are smoking fewer cigars, they are smoking better cigars and enjoying them more—and that's what counts.

But They're Not Just for Men...

Although today's American women cigar smokers often feel like they are pioneers, they aren't really breaking new ground. In earlier times, it was not unusual to see a woman

Demi Moore

smoke a cigar in the United States. First lady Dolly Madison didn't smoke cigars while in the White House—she enjoyed snuff. But First Lady Rachel Jackson was often seen smoking cigars by the fire with her husband, President Andrew Jackson. These precedents, however, were effectively buried by puritanically minded people who created a powerful prejudice against women smoking cigars. Cigars were considered unsanitary and were also branded as too masculine. (At the time, cigarettes were considered more feminine.)

Once established, the taboo against women smoking was tenacious. In 1845, Wilhelm de Lenz, a Russian nobleman visiting Paris, preferred to leave the room rather than deal with the sight of a woman, writer George Sand, smoking a cigar. Even worse, a French officer who probably considered himself well-mannered, General Galliffet, would approach a woman who dared light a cigar in his presence and suggest that they go visit the men's room together.

While men may have recoiled when women lit up—and despite what some women suspect—the taboo was not the

Whoopi Goldberg

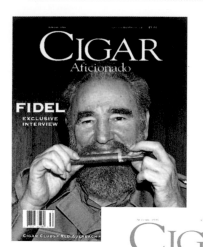

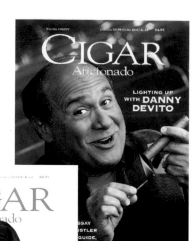

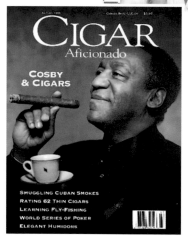

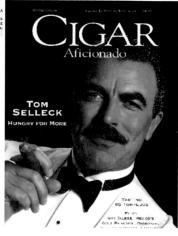

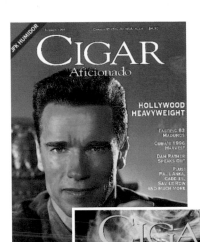

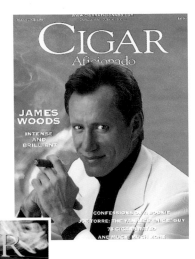

result of a conspiracy of men who wanted to keep cigars for themselves. Plenty of women were involved in creating an image of femininity that didn't include cigars. The same female social reformers who taught women immigrants to America that they needed to bathe more often also urged them to eschew tobacco.

In spite of the reformers, there have always been a few brave cigar-smoking ladies, but most of them smoked in private. Even into the 1980s, women were more likely to be selling cigars (as in the women, including Susan Anton, who sold Muriels) than smoking them. Somehow the gender revolution and general hedonism of the 60s and 70s didn't afford women an equal right to enjoy fine tobacco. Instead, some outspoken women (and quite a few men) feel empowered to censure anyone who dares smoke in public, and many wives demonstrate their domestic authority by forbidding all smoking in their homes.

Rachel Jackson's cigar would be quite unwelcome in today's White House: Hillary Rodham Clinton forbids smoking there. But, elsewhere in the 1990s, legions of women are challenging the old stereotypes by proudly lighting up in public. In Europe, in particular, it has become common to see a well-dressed woman smoking a cigar. In America, however, there is a lingering bias which says that cigar smoking just isn't feminine and which leads—even today—to crude "Freudian" comments by unimaginative boors who inevitably see a cigar as a phallic symbol.

The sight of a woman smoking still grabs attention, and American advertisers and filmmakers are taking full advantage of this. A host of ads and articles feature women who seem a bit rebellious, different, and perhaps even naughty, just because they are puffing on a cigar. The 1996 Hollywood hit *The First Wives Club* is a good example: the movie's ad campaign featured Bette Midler, Goldie Hawn, and Diane Keaton—as women seeking revenge on ex-husbands who left them for "trophy wives"—proudly brandishing their stogies.

Marlene Dietrich ignored the taboo against women smokers.

Unquestionably, some women have taken up smoking because of the effect their smoking has on the opposite sex. For many men, the sight of a woman smoking a cigar is irresistibly sexy. At the very least, it's a great conversation starter. (Of course, in Madonna's hands, a cigar can be a conversation stopper. She effectively used her cigar as a prop when she decided she wanted to fluster her host during her notorious appearance on David Letterman's *Late Show*.) But, by the same measure, there are plenty of men for whom cigar smoking is an affectation, rather than an appreciation.

The growing number of women-only cigar dinners and events is proof that many women are smoking for pleasure and camaraderie, not just to attract or fluster men. The forces of reaction have no more chance of preventing women from smoking cigars than they do of keeping them from driving sports cars or running corporations.

There are still many more aficionados than aficionadas. But the ranks of cigar smoking women are swelling, as are the ranks of women in the cigar business. At this point, it is not just condescending for an experienced male smoker to try to educate a woman smoker about cigars (unless, of course, she asks); it is also downright foolish. There's a good chance that she knows as much about cigars as he does and may end up telling him a thing or two.

Some of the great cigar-smokin' mamas of the past included:

- Greta Garbo
- Colette
- Gertrude Stein
- Mae West
- Annie Oakley
- Amy Lowell
- Bonnie Parker
- Bette Davis
- George Sand (after whom cigar-smoking societies have been named)
- Marlene Dietrich (whose entrance in a movie wearing a man's suit and a cigar was once considered scandalous, and deliciously erotic) and
- Catherine the Great, who, according to legend, had cigar bands created to prevent her gloves from getting stained.

Today's list of well-known women who are not waiting to exhale includes:

- Jodie Foster
- Whoopi Goldberg
- Demi Moore
- Linda Evangelista
- Drew Barrymore
- Madonna
- Lauren Hutton
- Nicole Kidman
- Sharon Stone
- Jennifer Tilly
- Ellen Barkin
- Susan Powter
- Princess Margaret
- Anne Archer

Wisps of Smoking-Room Banter: Tall Tales, Legends, and Cigar Lore

Part of the pleasure of fine cigars is the lore and legends that surround them. Here are just a few samples, presented in random order. To hear more, just hang out at any fine cigar shop or read any issue of *Cigar Aficionado*.

Thomas Alva Edison. The great inventor tried to foil people who filched his Havanas by having fake cigars made of cabbage leaves rolled in brown paper. Unfortunately, he lost track of the real cigars and ended up smoking the fakes himself.

Thomas Edison: an experiment that backfired?

Casey Stengel. A Dodger named Cuccinello was tagged out when he disobeyed third-base coach Casey Stengel's shouts telling him to slide. He didn't slide because to do so would have broken the cigars in his pocket. Those who remember Stengel can imagine his reaction.

Rudyard Kipling. Kipling guaranteed his immortality with smokers, and offended countless women, by putting the following line in his poem *The Betrothed:* "And a woman is only a woman, but a good cigar is a smoke."

James Humes. U.S. Ambassador to Austria told the deputy chief of his mission to dispose of several boxes of Havana cigars

Sigmund Freud (seated at left) once said: "But a cigar can surely be just a cigar after all, you know?"

by saying, "Burn them . . . one by one . . . slowly." The story is also told about JFK and Pierre Salinger, and occasionally about JFK and Arthur Schlesinger.

George Burns. The comedian claimed he smoked cheap cigars because they didn't go out during his act the way good ones did.

Sigmund Freud. The founder of psychoanalysis was so fond of his cigars that he became almost irrational when he found he was without them. Other people said he was "defensive" about his smoking.

Catherine the Great of Russia. The story goes that this powerful empress had her cigars wrapped in silk to keep them from staining her fingers, and that this practice led to cigar bands. Unfortunately, it's an apocryphal tale. Credit for the invention of the band probably belongs to a factory owner named Gustave Bock.

Babe Ruth. When the Bambino was playing in Boston, before he came to the Yankees, he invested in a local cigar factory that manufactured a five-cent cigar with his picture on the band.

Melvin Laird. Richard Nixon's Secretary of Defense pocketed a lit cigar so as not to offend the Pope. His jacket caught on fire.

L. Frank Baum. The author of *The Wonderful Wizard of Oz* was often seen with an unlit cigar in his mouth. Once, while at the shore, he was asked about his habit. He explained that he lit them when he went into the water. Since he couldn't swim, he watched the cigar; when it went out, he was getting in too deep. He then walked into the water and demonstrated this practice. When he returned, he claimed that, "if it hadn't been for the cigar, I would have drowned."

Winston Churchill. The English statesman once hid from an appointment by telling his valet to answer the door and say Churchill was out and to smoke one of Churchill's cigars while doing so, so that the caller would believe that Churchill was really out.

Sibelius. The great Finnish composer benefitted greatly from his friendship with Churchill, who supplied him with cigars.

Groucho Marx. While hosting the show "You Bet Your Life," Groucho came across a Mrs. Story who explained having had twenty-two children by saying "I love my husband." He quipped, "I like my cigar, too, but I take it out of my mouth once in a while," but the comment was cut before the show was broadcast.

Napoleon III of France. On being asked to ban smoking, the Emperor replied, "This vice brings in one hundred million a year in taxes. I will certainly forbid it at once— as soon as you can name a virtue that brings in as much revenue."

Tip O'Neill. The Speaker of the House told Vice President Walter Mondale, "You better take advantage of the good cigars. You don't get much else in that job."

Francis Ford Coppola. The award-winning movie director carries a gold-and-silver cigar cutter that once belonged to Hollywood studio head Jack Warner. Before Warner, it belonged to Lord Mountbatten.

Oscar Hammerstein I. The Hammerstein who teamed up with Richard Rogers was the grandson of this earlier Oscar who invented a cigar-making machine, published a tobacco

Babe Ruth with bat and stick.

journal, and used his profits to build theaters.

Mark Twain. This oft-quoted cigar smoker once said that he wouldn't go to heaven if he couldn't smoke there.

Lenin. Zino Davidoff used to recount that one of the frequent visitors to his family's cigar shop in Kiev was a man named Vladimir Ulyanov, who later became known to the world as Lenin. He smoked cardboard-tipped "papirosi."

The Grateful Dead. Although this much-followed band

was generally suspected of smoking something other than cigars, fine cigars were often to be found in the backstage rooms at their concerts.

José Marti. In 1895, the legendary Cuban revolutionary sent the message to begin the uprising against Spanish rule to his associates rolled up inside a cigar.

George Sand. The notorious French (female) literary giant shocked society by dressing in men's clothing—and shocked her many male lovers by smoking huge cigars at breakfast.

Pancho Villa. This hard-riding Mexican bandit and rebel advised his men to smoke cigars after breakfast.

Edward VII of England. This royal aficionado suffered for years because his mother, Queen Victoria of England, hated cigars and forbade cigar smoking in her presence. When she died and he assumed the throne, he quickly declared, "Gentlemen, you may proceed to smoke."

Arthur Rubinstein. This famed piano genius was so fond of cigars that, at one point, he acquired a tobacco plantation in Cuba which produced cigars with his portrait on the band.

John Wayne. The Duke liked things big, so he smoked custom-made, larger-than-usual cigars.

Amy Lowell. When this well-known poet and critic suggested to a car mechanic that he call her brother, the President of Harvard University, as a reference, A.L. Lowell asked what the woman was doing at that moment. Told that she was smoking a big cigar, Lowell confirmed that it must be his sister.

Art Buchwald. The humorist is said to like cigars so much that he has smoked them while playing tennis.

Lord Byron. The famed poet wrote an ode to the cigar called "Sublime Tobacco."

Franz Liszt. The great 19th-century composer and concert pianist traveled with a huge humidor.

Calvin Coolidge. When a White House visitor asked the President for a cigar as a gift for a friend who collected cigar bands from famous smokers, Coolidge gave the visitor a band, but kept the cigar. Coolidge, not known as a spender, smoked good cigars when he received them as gifts, but he saved and reused a one-cent paper cigar holder.

Zino Davidoff. One of the greatest cigar experts of all time summed up his philosophy by saying, "The greatest cigar to smoke is the one you are currently smoking."

Rush Limbaugh. The controversial broadcaster didn't start smoking until in his 40s, but, once he discovered the pleasures of fine smoke, he quickly acquired twelve humidors.

John F. Kennedy. The charismatic young President had his trusted aide Pierre Salinger stockpile over 1,000 cigars just before he signed the Cuban embargo.

Elaine Kaufman. The proprietress of Elaine's, New York's fabled writers' hangout, would exile patrons who complained about cigar smoke to a side room nicknamed "Siberia."

Jefferson Davis. Before the War Between the States, the future president of the Confederacy would smoke cigars with his father-in-law, U.S. President Zachary Taylor.

Ulysses S. Grant. The war hero and President was almost always pictured with a cigar; he received so many cigars as gifts he had to give many away. His 1868 campaign song was "A-smokin' His Cigar."

Milton Hershey. Philanthropist and candy magnate Hershey was a notorious cigar smoker—eight to ten per day until he died at the age of 88. He had several sugar plantations and mills in Cuba and spent a great deal of time there. Every morning after breakfast in Cuba he walked to his production factory, The Sugar House, smoking a Corona-Corona. There were "No Smoking" signs at the door and Hershey would put his cigar on the windowsill when he entered. Without fail the cigar would have disappeared into the hands of a native by the time he returned.

Dan Rather. The respected network news anchor was given one Cuban cigar by Fidel Castro in 1979. Rather brought it back from Cuba hidden from authorities who never found it—or, as Rather puts it, they might have found it but said, "What the hell, let Dan have one good cigar."

Oscar Hammerstein I. The grandfather of Oscar II—the famous Broadway lyricist—was a renowned opera manager and major influence on the development of the Broadway theater district, but his real life's passion was cigars. He invented a cigar-making machine that revolutionized tobacco processing, and personally hand-rolled 25 cigars a day for his own consumption. The capital from Hammerstein's extremely profitable cigar endeavors financed his theater-building ambitions. So it is said that cigars built Times Square.

William Jefferson Clinton. The President does not smoke cigars in public, and there is ongoing controversy as to whether he smokes them in private. But it is well known that he *chews* cigars on the golf course.

CIGAR BRAND DIRECTORY

<table>
<tr><td colspan="2" align="center">LEGEND</td></tr>
<tr><td>AL CAPONE</td><td>Brand</td></tr>
<tr><td>Nicaragua</td><td>Country of Manufacture</td></tr>
<tr><td>C/D</td><td>Strength Key: A = Mild, B = Mild to Medium, C = Medium,
D = Medium to Strong, E = Strong</td></tr>
<tr><td>Nestor Plasencia</td><td>Manufacturer</td></tr>
<tr><td>Corona Grande</td><td>Cigar Name</td></tr>
<tr><td>6¾"</td><td>Length</td></tr>
<tr><td>43</td><td>Ring Gauge</td></tr>
<tr><td>83</td><td>Cigar Aficionado Rating (based on 50 to 100 scale)</td></tr>
</table>

	SIZE	RATING
AL CAPONE		
Nicaragua C/D		
Nestor Plasencia		
Corona Grande	6¾" x 43	83
Robusto	4¾" x 50	
AROMAS DE SAN ANDRES		
Mexico B		
Tabacos Santa Clara		
Aficionado	6" x 50	
Aficionado Maduro	6" x 50	
Gourmet Tube	6⅛" x 42	
Maxmillian	7½" x 52	
Maxmillian Maduro	7½" x 52	
Robusto	5" x 50	83
Robusto Maduro	5" x 50	
ARTURO FUENTE		
Dominican Republic D		
Tabacalera A. Fuente y Cia.		
Brevas Royale	5½" x 42	
Brevas Royale Maduro	5½" x 42	
Cañones	8½" x 52	
Cañones Maduro	8½" x 52	
Chateau Fuente	4½" x 50	85
Chateau Fuente Robusto	6" x 50	88
Chateau Fuente Royal Salute	7⅝" x 54	86
Chateau Fuente Royal Salute Maduro	7⅝" x 54	
Churchill	7¼" x 48	89
Churchill Maduro	7" x 48	85
Corona Imperial	6½" x 46	
Corona Imperial Maduro	6½" x 46	86
Cuban Corona	5¼" x 45	
Cuban Corona Maduro	5¼" x 45	
Curly Head	6½" x 43	
Curly Head Maduro	6½" x 43	

	SIZE	RATING
Curly Head Deluxe	6½" x 43	
Curly Head Deluxe Maduro	6½" x 43	
Dantes	7" x 52	
Dantes Maduro	6⅞" x 49	
Don Carlos #3	5½" x 44	90
Don Carlos Robusto	5" x 50	87
Double Chateau Fuente	6¾" x 50	89
Double Chateau Fuente Maduro	6¾" x 50	
8-5-8	6" x 47	86
Flor Fina 8-5-8	6" x 47	86
Fumas	7" x 44	
Fumas Maduro	7" x 44	
Hemingway Classic	7" x 48	86
Hemingway Masterpiece	9¼" x 52	86
Hemingway Short Story	4¼" x 48	89
Hemingway Signature	6" x 47	89
Panatela Fina	7" x 38	85
Panatela Fina Maduro	7" x 38	
Petit Corona	5" x 38	86
Petit Corona Maduro	7" x 38	
Rothschild	4½" x 50	86
Rothschild Maduro	4½" x 50	
Selección d'Or Churchill	7¼" x 48	
Selección d'Or Corona Imperial	6½" x 46	
Selección d'Or Privada #1	6¾" x 44	85
Spanish Lonsdale	6½" x 42	88
Spanish Lonsdale Maduro	6½" x 42	
ASHTON		
Dominican Republic D		
Tabacalera A. Fuente y Cia.		
Aged Maduro #10	5" x 50	83
Aged Maduro #20	5½" x 44	86
Aged Maduro #30	6¾" x 44	87

Strength Key: A = Mild, **B** = Mild to Medium, **C** = Medium, **D** = Medium to Strong, **E** = Strong

	SIZE	RATING
Aged Maduro #40	6" x 50	**85**
Aged Maduro #50	7" x 48	**86**
Aged Maduro #60	7½" x 52	**84**
Cabinet Selection #1	9" x 52	**87**
Cabinet Selection #2	7" x 46	**87**
Cabinet Selection #3	6" x 46	**88**
Cabinet Selection #6	5½" x 52	**87**
Cabinet Selection #7	6¼" x 52	**88**
Cabinet Selection #8	7" x 49	
Cabinet Selection #10	7½" x 52	**89**
Churchill	7½" x 52	**85**
Cordial	5" x 30	**85**
Corona	5½" x 44	**84**
Double Magnum	6" x 50	**87**
8-9-8	6½" x 44	**86**
Elegante	6½" x 35	**82**
Magnum	5" x 50	**87**
Panatela	6" x 36	**84**
Prime Minister	6⅞" x 48	**84**

Astral
Honduras **C**
UST International Inc.

Besos	5" x 52	**89**
Favorito	7" x 48	**83**
Lujos	6½" x 44	**84**
Maestro	7½" x 52	
Perfeccion	7" x 48	**85**

Avo
Dominican Republic **D**
Tabacos Dominicanos S.A.

Belicoso	6" x 50	**87**
No. 1	6⅔" x 42	**86**
No. 2	6" x 50	**88**
No. 3	7½" x 52	**84**
No. 4	7" x 38	**81**
No. 5	6¾" x 46	**87**
No. 6	6½" x 36	**88**
No. 7	6" x 44	**87**
No. 8	5½" x 40	**87**
No. 9	4¾" x 48	**83**
Petit Belicoso	4¾" x 50	**86**
Pyramid	7" x 54	**86**

Avo XO
Dominican Republic **D**
Tabacos Dominicanos S.A.

Intermezzo	5½" x 50	**83**
Maestoso	7" x 48	**86**
Preludio	6" x 40	**87**

Baccarat Havana Selection
Honduras **C**
Agroindustrias Laepe

Bonita	4½" x 30	
Churchill	7" x 48	**84**

	SIZE	RATING
Churchill Maduro	7" x 50	**85**
Luchadores	6" x 43	**83**
No. 1	7" x 44	**80**
Panatela	6" x 38	**81**
Petit Corona	5½" x 42	**87**
Platinum	4⅞" x 32	
Polo	7" x 52	
Robusto	5" x 50	**84**
Rothschild	5" x 50	**82**
Rothschild Maduro	5" x 50	

Bahia
Costa Rica **B/C**
Tony Borhani Cigars

Churchill	6⅞" x 48	
Double Corona	8" x 50	
Esplendido	6" x 50	
No. 3	6" x 46	
No. 4	5½" x 42	
Robusto	5" x 50	

Ballena Suprema
Honduras **B**
Consolidated Cigar Corp.

No. 744D Ventaja	7" x 44	
No. 747D Alma	7" x 47	
No. 754D Capitán	7" x 54	
No. 850D Encanto	8" x 50	

Bances
Honduras **C**
Villazon & Co.

Brevas	5½" x 43	**86**
Brevas Maduro	5½" x 43	
Cazadores	6¼" x 43	**78**
Cazadores Maduro	6¼" x 43	
Corona Inmensa	6¾" x 48	**87**
Crown	4" x 35	
Crown Maduro	5¾" x 50	
Demi Tasse Maduro	4" x 35	
El Prado Maduro	6¼" x 36	
Havana Holder	6½" x 30	
No. 1	n/a x n/a	
Palma	6" x 42	
President	8½" x 52	**89**
Unique	5½" x 38	**81**

Bauza
Dominican Republic **D**
Tabacalera A. Fuente y Cia.

Casa Grande	6¾" x 48	**84**
Fabuloso	7½" x 50	**86**
Florete	6⅞" x 35	**82**
Grecos	5½" x 42	**85**
Jaguar	6½" x 42	**83**
Medaille D'Oro No. 1	6⅞" x 44	**86**
Petit Corona	5" x 38	**84**

	SIZE	RATING
Presidente	7½" x 50	
Robusto	5½" x 50	**87**

BELINDA
Honduras **C**
Villazon & Co.

Ammo Box	6" x 44	
Ammo Box Maduro	6" x 44	
Belinda	6½" x 36	**87**
Brevas a la Conserva	5½" x 43	**87**
Cabinet	5⅝" x 45	**85**
Corona Grande	6¼" x 44	**85**
Excellente	6" x 50	**84**
Excellente Maduro	6" x 50	
Glass Humidor	6" x 43	
Medaglia d'Oro	4½" x 50	**84**
Mina	5⅜" x 28	
Prime Minister	7½" x 50	**91**
Prime Minister Maduro	7½" x 50	
Ramon	7¼" x 47	
Robusto en Cedro	4½" x 50	
Robusto en Cedro Maduro	4½" x 50	

BERING
Honduras **B**
Nestor Plasencia

Baron	7¼" x 42	**86**
Baron Maduro	7¼" x 42	
Casino	7⅛" x 42	**79**
Cazadores	6¼" x 45	
Corona Grande	6¼" x 46	**83**
Corona Royale	6" x 41	**87**
Coronado	5³⁄₁₆" x 45	**85**
Gold #1	6¼" x 33	**83**
Grande Wood	8½" x 52	
Hispanos	6" x 50	**85**
Hispanos Maduro	6" x 50	
Imperial	5¼" x 42	**84**
Inmensa	7⅛" x 45	
Inmensa Maduro	7⅛" x 45	
Plazas	6" x 43	**87**
Robusto	4¾" x 50	**80**
Torpedo	7" x 54	

BOLIVAR
Cuba **D**

Belicoso Fino	5½" x 52	**90**
Bonitas	4⅞" x 40	
Corona	5½" x 42	**91**
Corona Extra	5¾" x 46	**87**
Corona Gigantes	7" x 47	**90**
Corona Junior	5⅓" x 42	
Demi Tasse	4" x 30	
Gold Medal	6½" x 42	**90**
Inmensa	6⅔" x 43	**87**
Lonsdales	6½" x 42	

	SIZE	RATING
Palmas	7" x 33	
Petit Corona	5" x 42	**87**
Regentes	4⅞" x 34	
Royal Coronas	5" x 50	**95**
Suprema Churchill	7" x 47	

C.A.O.
Honduras **C**
Nestor Plasencia

Churchill	8" x 50	
Churchill Maduro	8" x 50	**85**
Corona	6" x 42	**87**
Corona Maduro	6" x 42	
Corona Gorda	6" x 50	**85**
Corona Gorda Maduro	6" x 50	
Lonsdale	7" x 44	**85**
Petit Corona	5" x 40	
Presidente	7½" x 54	
Presidente Maduro	7½" x 54	
Robusto	4½" x 50	**86**
Robusto Maduro	4½" x 50	**84**
Triangulare	7" x 54	**86**
Triangulare Maduro	7" x 54	

C.A.O. GOLD
Nicaragua **C**
Nestor Plasencia

Churchill	7" x 48	
Corona	5½" x 42	
Corona Gorda	6½" x 50	**86**
Double Corona	7½" x 54	
Robusto	5" x 50	**89**

CABALLEROS
Dominican Republic **C**
Manufactura de Tabacos S.A. de C.V.

Churchill	7" x 50	**85**
Corona	5¾" x 43	**83**
Double Corona	6¾" x 48	
Petit Corona	5½" x 42	
Rothschild	5" x 50	**82**

CABAÑAS
Dominican Republic **C**
Consolidated Cigar Corp.

Corona	5½" x 42	**84**
Exquisito Maduro	6½" x 48	**84**
Premiers	6⅝" x 42	
Royale	5⅝" x 46	**83**

CACIQUE
Dominican Republic **C**
Tabacos Dominicanos S.A.

Apache	6" x 50	**81**
Apache Maduro	6" x 50	
Azteca	4¾" x 50	
Azteca Maduro	4¾" x 50	

Strength Key: A = Mild, **B** = Mild to Medium, **C** = Medium, **D** = Medium to Strong, **E** = Strong

	SIZE	RATING
Caribes	6⅞" x 46	
Incas	7½" x 50	
Jaragua	6¾" x 36	
No. 3	6¾" x 36	82
No. 7	6⅞" x 46	86
Siboneyes	6¾" x 43	
Tainos	6" x 42	

CALIXTO LOPEZ
Philippines   C
La Flor de la Isabella, Inc.

Corona Exquisto	5⅜" x 43	
Corona Numero 1	6⅝" x 45	
Czars	8" x 45	
Gigantes	8½" x 50	
Lonsdale Suprema	6¾" x 42	
Palma Royale	7¼" x 36	

CALLE OCHO
U.S.A. & Dominican Republic   C
Caribbean Cigar Co.

Churchill	7¼" x 50	
Doble	7½" x 46	
Embajador	9" x 60	81
Festivale	5½" x 44	
Gordito	5" x 50	85
Gordito Largo	6" x 50	80
Immenso	7½" x 54	
Laguito	7½" x 38	
Niñas	5" x 38	
Perfect Corona	6½" x 42	
Pyramid	7¼" x 54	
Torpedo	6½" x 54	

CAMACHO
Honduras   C
Caribe Imported Cigars Inc.

Cazadores	6½" x 44	
Cetros	6½" x 44	
Cetros Maduro	6½" x 44	
Churchill	7" x 48	85
Churchill Maduro	7" x 48	
Conchitas	5½" x 32	
Conchitas Maduro	5½" x 32	
El Cesar	8½" x 52	
El Cesar Maduro	8½" x 52	
Elegante	6⅛" x 38	
Elegante Maduro	6⅛" x 38	
Executive	7¾" x 50	
Executive Maduro	7¾" x 50	
Monarca	5" x 50	82
Monarca Maduro	5" x 50	
Nacionales	5½" x 44	85
Nacionales Maduro	5½" x 44	
No. 1	7" x 44	76
No. 1 Maduro	7" x 44	
Palmas	6" x 43	

	SIZE	RATING
Palmas Maduro	6" x 43	
Pan Especial	7" x 36	
Pan Especial Maduro	7" x 36	

CAMÓRRA
Honduras   C
Justo Eiroa

Capri	5½" x 32	85
Genova	5½" x 44	
Napoli	6⅛" x 38	
Padova	5" x 44	
Roma	5" x 50	81
San Remo	7" x 48	
Venizia	6½" x 44	

CANARIA D'ORO
Dominican Republic   C
General Cigar Co.

Babies	4¼" x 32	
Corona	5½" x 43	84
Fino	6" x 31	84
Inmenso	5½" x 49	83
Lonsdale	5½" x 43	83
Rothschild	4½" x 50	88
Rothschild Maduro	4½" x 49	86
Supremo	7" x 45	85

CANONERO
Brazil   A
Menendez Amerino & Cia. Ltda.

#1 Double Corona	7½" x 50	
#2 Rothschild	5½" x 50	
#3 Robusto	5" x 52	
#4 Churchill	7" x 46	
#10 Lonsdale	6½" x 42	
#20 Corona	5½" x 42	
#30 Petit	4¼" x 38	

CARLOS TURANO
Dominican Republic   C
Cuervo y Hermano

Carlos I	6" x 50	
Carlos II	6¾" x 43	
Carlos III	7½" x 52	
Carlos IV	5¾" x 43	
Carlos V	6" x 46	
Carlos VI	7" x 48	
Carlos VII	4¾" x 52	
Carlos VIII	6½" x 36	

CARMEN
Honduras   n/a
Carmen

Churchill	7" x 48	
Corona	5¾" x 43	
Presidente	7¾" x 50	
Pyramid	6½" x 58	

	SIZE	RATING
Robusto	4¾" x 52	
Toro	6" x 50	

CARRINGTON
Dominican Republic   **B**
**Tabacos Dominicanos S.A. & Puros
de Villa Gonzalez S.A.**

	SIZE	RATING
I	7½" x 50	
II	6" x 42	87
III	7" x 36	85
IV	5½" x 40	80
V	6⅞" x 46	87
VI	4½" x 50	78
VII	6" x 50	79
VIII	6⅞" x 60	87

CASA BLANCA
Dominican Republic   **C**
Manufactura de Tabacos S.A. de C.V.

Bonita	4" x 36	
Corona	5½" x 42	89
Deluxe	6" x 50	85˙
Deluxe Maduro	6" x 50	87
Half Jeroboam	5" x 66	
Half Jeroboam Maduro	5" x 66	
Jeroboam	10" x 66	86
Jeroboam Maduro	10" x 66	
Lonsdale	6½" x 42	84
Lonsdale Maduro	6½" x 42	
Magnum	7" x 60	
Magnum Maduro	7" x 60	
Panatela	6" x 36	84
Presidente	7½" x 50	84
Presidente Maduro	7½" x 50	83

CELESTINO VEGA
Indonesia   **C**
Caribbean Cigar Co.

Borobudur	3⅝" x 20	
Corona	4¾" x 40	
Half Corona	4½" x 36	
Panatela	5" x 32	
Senorita	4⅛" x 32	
Slim Panatela	7" x 28	
The Cuban	8¼" x 48	

CERDAN
Dominican Republic   **B**
Tabacos Dominicanos S.A.

Chamberlain	6" x 43	
Churchill	7" x 45	
Don Juan	7½" x 50	
Don Julio	6½" x 54	
Ejecutivos	5½" x 38	
Gable	7½" x 38	
Gemma's	6" x 30	
Juan Carlos	7" x 35	

	SIZE	RATING
Napolean	5½" x 40	
Welles	6¾" x 40	

CHURCHILL
Honduras   **n/a**
Nestor Plasencia

No. 3	5⅝" x 44	
Presidente	8" x 50	
Prime Minister	7¼" x 48	
Robusto	4¾" x 50	
Senator	6" x 50	

CIFUENTES BY PARTAGAS
Jamaica   **C**
General Cigar Co.

Churchill	7½" x 49	90
Corona Gorda	5½" x 49	88
Lonsdale	6½" x 42	83
Petit Corona	5" x 38	86
Pyramid	6" x 50	

COHIBA
Cuba   **E**

Corona Especial	6" x 38	89
Esplendidos	7" x 47	89
Exquisitos	4⅞" x 33	
Lancero	7" x 38	83
Panatela	4½" x 26	
Robusto	5" x 50	91
Siglo I	4" x 40	93
Siglo II	5" x 42	88
Siglo III	6" x 42	95
Siglo IV	6" x 46	89
Siglo V	6¾" x 43	90

COHIBA
Dominican Republic   **D**
General Cigar Co.

Coronas Especial	6¼" x 43	
Esplendido	7" x 49	
Robusto	5½" x 48	

CREDO
Dominican Republic   **B/C**
Manufactura de Tabacos S.A. de C.V.

Arcane	5" x 50	86
Athanor	5¾" x 42	88
Jubilate	5" x 34	83
Magnificat	6⅞" x 46	84
Pythagoras	7" x 50	

CRUZ REAL
Mexico   **C**
**Tabacos y Puros de San Andres S.A.
de C.V.**

Canciler	7½" x 50	
Churchill No.14	7½" x 50	87

Strength Key: A = Mild, **B** = Mild to Medium, **C** = Medium, **D** = Medium to Strong, **E** = Strong

	SIZE	RATING
Emperador	6¼" x 50	
Ministro	6¼" x 42	
No. 1	6⅝" x 42	**76**
No. 1 Maduro	6⅝" x 42	
No. 2	6" x 42	**86**
No. 2 Maduro	6" x 42	
No. 3	6⅝" x 35	
No. 3 Maduro	6⅝" x 34	
No. 14	7½" x 50	**87**
No. 14 Maduro	7½" x 50	
No. 19	6" x 50	**80**
No. 19 Maduro	6" x 50	**84**
No. 24	4½" x 50	**80**
No. 24 Maduro	4½" x 50	
No. 25	5½" x 52	**77**
No. 25 Maduro	5½" x 52	
No. 28	8½" x 54	**82**
No. 28 Maduro	8½" x 54	

CUABA

Cuba **D**

Divinos	4" x 43	
Exclusivos	5" x 46	
Generosos	5⅛" x 42	
Tradiciónales	4¾" x 42	**91**

CUBA ALIADOS

Honduras **D**

Cuba Aliados Cigars, Inc.

Churchill	7¼" x 54	**92**
Churchill Deluxe	7¼" x 54	**88**
Churchill Extra	7¼" x 54	**84**
Corona Deluxe	6½" x 45	**87**
Lonsdale	6½" x 42	**91**
No. 4	5½" x 46	**87**
Pyramide	7½" x 60	**87**
Pyramide No. 2	6½" x 46	**89**
Remedios	5½" x 42	**86**
Rothschild	5" x 50	**84**
Valentino No. 1	7" x 47	**89**

CUBITA

Dominican Republic **C**

Manufactura de Tabacos S.A. de C.V.

2	6¼" x 38	**85**
2000	7" x 50	**82**
500	5½" x 43	
700	6" x 50	**86**
8-9-8	6¾" x 43	**83**
Delicias	5⅛" x 30	

CUESTA-REY

Dominican Republic **C**

Tabacalera A. Fuente y Cia.

	SIZE	RATING
Aristocrat	7¼" x 48	
Cabinet Selection No. 1	8½" x 52	
Cabinet Selection No. 1 Maduro	8½" x 52	
Cabinet Selection No. 2	7" x 36	**87**
Cabinet Selection No. 2 Maduro	7" x 36	
Cabinet Selection No. 1884	6¾" x 44	**85**
Cabinet Selection No. 1884 Maduro	6¾" x 44	**88**
Cabinet Selection No. 8-9-8	7" x 49	**86**
Cabinet Selection No. 8-9-8 Maduro	7" x 49	
Cabinet Selection No. 95	6¼" x 42	**84**
Cabinet Selection No. 95 Maduro	6¼" x 42	**85**
Cameo	4¼" x 32	
Centennial Collection Captiva	6$\frac{3}{16}$" x 42	**84**
Centennial Collection Dominican No. 1	8½" x 52	
Centennial Collection Dominican No. 1 Maduro	8½" x 50	
Centennial Collection Dominican No. 2	7¼" x 48	**84**
Centennial Collection Dominican No. 2 Maduro	7¼" x 48	**87**
Centennial Collection Dominican No. 3	7" x 36	**86**
Centennial Collection Dominican No. 3 Maduro	7" x 36	
Centennial Collection Dominican No. 4	6¼" x 42	**83**
Centennial Collection Dominican No. 4 Maduro	6½" x 42	
Centennial Collection Dominican No. 5	5½" x 43	**87**
Centennial Collection Dominican No. 5 Maduro	5½" x 43	
Centennial Collection Dominican No. 60	6" x 50	**87**
Centennial Collection Dominican No. 7	4½" x 50	**84**
Individual Natural	8½" x 52	

DAVIDOFF

Dominican Republic **D**

Tabacos Dominicanos S.A.

2000	5" x 42	**85**
4000	6" x 42	**89**
5000	5⅝" x 46	**85**
Aniversario No. 1	7½" x 38	**82**

	SIZE	RATING
Aniversario No. 2	7" x 48	86
Double "R"	7½" x 50	92
Gran Cru No. 1	6" x 42	89
Gran Cru No. 2	5⅝" x 43	88
Gran Cru No. 3	5" x 42	88
Gran Cru No. 4	5" x 40	88
No. 1	7½" x 38	83
No. 2	6" x 38	86
No. 3	5⅛" x 30	81
Special "C"	6½" x 33	
Special "R"	4⅞" x 50	87
Special "T"	6" x 52	87

DIAMOND CROWN
Dominican Republic   **D**
Tabacalera A. Fuente y Cia.

Robusto No. 1	8½" x 54	86
Robusto No. 2	7½" x 54	
Robusto No. 3	6½" x 54	
Robusto No. 4	5½" x 54	90
Robusto No. 5	4½" x 54	87

**DIANA SILVIUS DIAMOND
VINTAGE SELECTION**
Dominican Republic   **C**
Tabacalera A. Fuente y Cia.

Churchill	7" x 50	88
Corona	6½" x 42	84
Diana 2000	6¾" x 46	
Robusto	4⅞" x 52	86

DIPLOMATICOS
Cuba   **C**

No. 1	6½" x 42	
No. 2	6⅛" x 52	92
No. 3	5½" x 42	
No. 4	5" x 42	
No. 5	4" x 40	
No. 6	7½" x 38	
No. 7	6" x 38	

DON ASA
Honduras   **B**
N/A

Blunts	5" x 42	
Cetros No. 2	6½" x 44	85
Corona	5½" x 50	85
Imperial	8" x 44	
President	7½" x 50	
Rothschild	4½" x 50	

DON DIEGO
Dominican Republic   **C**
Consolidated Cigar Corp.

Amigo	6½" x 36	
Babies	5¹⁄₁₆" x 36	75
Corona	5⅝" x 42	85

	SIZE	RATING
Corona Major Tube	5¹⁄₁₆" x 42	87
Coronas Brevas	6½" x 48	
Grande	6" x 50	84
Greco	6½" x 38	
Imperial	7⁵⁄₁₆" x 46	
Lonsdale	6⅝" x 42	86
Monarch	7" x 45	86
Petit Corona	5⅛" x 42	86
Preludes	4" x 28	
Privada No. 1	6⅝" x 43	87
Royal Palmas	6⅛" x 35	82

DON JUAN
Nicaragua   **D**
Nestor Plasencia

Cetro	6" x 43	80
Churchill	7" x 49	90
Lindas	5½" x 38	77
Matador	6" x 50	
Numero Uno	6⅝" x 44	84
Palma Fina	6⅞" x 36	
Presidente	8½" x 50	88
Robusto	5" x 50	87

DON LEO
Dominican Republic   **B**
Puros de Villa Gonzalez S.A.

Churchill	7½" x 50	
Corona	6½" x 44	
Double Corona	7" x 48	
Petit Corona	5½" x 42	
Presidente	8" x 52	
Robusto	5½" x 50	87
Rothschild	4½" x 50	
Toro	6¼" x 52	
Torpedo	6¾" x 52	

DON LINO
Honduras   **B**
Delos Reyes Cigar S.A.

Churchill	7" x 50	90
Colorado	5½" x 50	85
Colorado Deluxe Lonsdale	6½" x 44	
Colorado Deluxe Presidente	7½" x 50	84
Colorado Deluxe Robustos	5½" x 50	
Colorado Rothschild	4½" x 50	86
Colorado Torpedo	7" x 48	83
Havana Reserve Toro	5½" x 46	88

DON MARCOS
Dominican Republic   **B**
Consolidated Cigar Corp.

Cetros	6½" x 42	
Coronas	5½" x 42	

Strength Key: A = Mild, **B** = Mild to Medium, **C** = Medium, **D** = Medium to Strong, **E** = Strong

	SIZE	RATING
Double Corona	6½" x 48	
Monarch	7" x 46	
Naturals Tube	6" x 38	
Toros	6" x 50	85
Torpedos	6" x 50	

DON MATEO
Honduras   C
Nestor Plasencia

	SIZE	RATING
4¾" X 50	4¾" x 50	
5½" X 44	5½" x 44	
6¼" X 50	6¼" x 50	
6⅝" X 44	6⅝" x 44	
6⅞" X 48	6⅞" x 48	
8" X 50	8" x 50	

DON MELO
Honduras   C
Cigars of Honduras

	SIZE	RATING
Churchill	7" x 49	
Corona Extra	5½" x 46	86
Corona Gorda	6¼" x 44	86
Cremas	4½" x 42	
Nom Plus	4¾" x 50	85
Numero Dos	6" x 42	
Petit Corona	5½" x 42	85
Presidente	8½" x 50	

DON PEPE
Honduras   D/C
Suerdieck

	SIZE	RATING
Double Corona	7½" x 50	
Half Corona	4½" x 42	
Petit Lonsdale	6" x 42	
Robusto	5" x 50	
Slim Panatela	5¼" x 30	

DON TITO
U.S.A.   C
Cigar Par Excellence

	SIZE	RATING
Charlemagne	7¼" x 54	
Churchill	7" x 50	
Corona Gorda	6" x 52	
Coronas Extra Larga	7¾" x 44	
Double Corona	7¾" x 49	
Medaille d'Or No. 1	6¾" x 43	
Medaille d'Or No. 2	6¼" x 43	
Panatela	6⅞" x 37	80
Panatela Deluxe	7" x 37	
Pyramide	7¼" x 50	
Robusto	5" x 50	
Soberano	8" x 52	
Taino	6¼" x 46	
Torpedo No. 1	6½" x 54	

DON TOMÁS
Honduras   C
UST International Inc.

	SIZE	RATING
Blunt	5" x 42	86
Blunt Maduro	5" x 42	
Cetros #2	6½" x 44	83
Cetros #2 Maduro	6½" x 44	
Corona	5½" x 50	86
Corona Grande	6½" x 44	84
Corona Grande Maduro	6½" x 44	
Corona Grande 3's	6½" x 44	
Corona Grande Upright 20's	6½" x 44	
Corona Maduro	5½" x 42	
Elegante 3's	6" x 36	
Epicure	4½" x 32	
Epicure Maduro	4½" x 32	
Gigante 10's	8½" x 52	
Gigante 10's Maduro	8½" x 52	
Imperial	8" x 44	
Imperial Maduro	8" x 44	
International #1	6½" x 44	
International #2	5½" x 50	83
International #3	5½" x 42	
International #4	7" x 36	78
Matador	5½" x 42	87
Matador Maduro	5½" x 42	
Panatela Larga Maduro	7" x 38	85
Panatela	6" x 36	84
Panatela Larga	7" x 36	
Panatela Maduro	6" x 36	
Petit Corona 3's	5½" x 42	
Presidentes	7½" x 50	
Presidentes Maduro	7½" x 50	85
Rothschild	4½" x 50	80
Rothschild Maduro	4½" x 50	
Special Edition #100	7½" x 50	
Special Edition #200	6½" x 44	85
Special Edition #300	5" x 50	80
Special Edition #400	7" x 36	86
Special Edition #500	5½" x 46	87
Supremo	6¼" x 42	88
Supremo Maduro	6¼" x 42	
Toro	5½" x 46	84
Toro Maduro	5½" x 46	84

DON XAVIER
Canary Islands   C
Commercial Arico AL

	SIZE	RATING
Churchill	7½" x 50	
Corona	5⅝" x 46	83
Lonsdale	6⅝" x 42	84
Panatela	5⅝" x 39	
Robusto	4⅝" x 50	84

	SIZE	RATING
DOUBLE HAPPINESS		
Philippines **C**		
La Flor de la Isabella, Inc.		
Bliss	5¼" x 48	
Ecstasy	7" x 47	
Euphoria	6½" x 50	
Nirvana	6" x 52	
Rapture	5" x 50	
DUNHILL		
Canary Islands **C**		
Citas Tabacos de Canarias S.A.		
Aged 1989 Panatela	6" x 36	**84**
Coronas	5½" x 43	
Coronas Extra	5½" x 50	**83**
Coronas Grandes	6½" x 43	
Lonsdale Grandes	7½" x 42	
Panatela	6" x 30	**81**
DUNHILL AGED 1989		
Dominican Republic **C/D**		
Consolidated Cigar Corp.		
Altamira	5" x 48	**88**
Cabreras	7" x 48	**86**
Caleta	4" x 40	
Centenas	6" x 50	**82**
Condados	6" x 48	**85**
Diamantes	6⅝" x 42	**83**
Fantino	7" x 28	**83**
Peravias	7" x 50	**87**
Romanas Vintage	4½" x 50	**87**
Samanas	6½" x 38	
Tabaras	5½" x 42	**85**
Valverdes	5 9/16" x 42	**85**
DUNHILL AGED 1994		
Dominican Republic **C/D**		
Consolidated Cigar Corp.		
Altamiras	5" x 48	**82**
Cabreras	7" x 48	
Centenas	6" x 50	
Condados	6" x 48	
Diamantes	6⅝" x 42	
Peravias	7" x 50	
Romanos	4½" x 50	
Samanas	6½" x 38	
8-9-8 COLLECTION		
Jamaica **B**		
General Cigar Co.		
Churchill	7½" x 49	**87**
Corona	5½" x 42	**88**
Lonsdale	6½" x 42	**86**
Monarch	6¾" x 45	**86**
Robusto	5½" x 49	**87**

	SIZE	RATING
EL REY DEL MUNDO		
Cuba **B/C**		
Choix Supreme	5" x 48	
Corona	5½" x 42	
Coronas De Luxe	5½" x 42	**91**
Demi Tasse	4" x 30	
Elegante	6¾" x 28	**83**
Gran Corona	5⅝" x 46	**87**
Grandes De España	7½" x 38	**88**
Isabel	5⅝" x 35	
Lonsdale	6½" x 42	**87**
Lunch Club	4½" x 40	
Panatelas Largas	7" x 28	
Petit Corona	5" x 42	
Petit Lonsdale	5" x 42	
Señoritas	4½" x 26	
Tainos	7" x 47	**87**
Trés Petit Corona	4" x 40	
EL REY DEL MUNDO		
Honduras **C/D**		
Villazon & Co.		
Cafe Au Lait	4½" x 35	
Cedar	7" x 43	
Choix Supreme	6" x 49	**88**
Classic Cofradias	6¼" x 48	
Classic Corona	5¾" x 45	
Corona Inmensa	7¼" x 47	
Corona Inmensa Maduro	7¼" x 47	
Corona	5⅝" x 45	**82**
Coronation	8½" x 52	
Double Corona	7" x 49	**86**
Elegantes	5⅜" x 29	
Flor de La Vonda	6½" x 42	**85**
Flor de Llaneza	6½" x 54	**87**
Flor del Mundo	7½" x 54	**87**
Habana Club	5½" x 42	**87**
Imperiales	7¼" x 54	
Lonsdale	7" x 43	**87**
Monte Carlo	6¼" x 50	
Olivas	n/a x n/a	
Originale	5⅝" x 45	**89**
Petit Lonsdale	4½" x 43	
Plantations	6½" x 30	
Principales	8" x 47	
Rectangulare	5⅝" x 45	**84**
Reynitas	5" x 38	
Robusto	5" x 54	**83**
Robusto de Manuel	5" x 54	**82**
Robusto Larga	6" x 54	**83**
Robusto Maduro	5" x 54	
Robusto Suprema	7" x 54	**91**
Robusto Zavalla	5" x 54	**81**
Rothschild	5" x 50	**86**
Tinos	5½" x 38	**87**
Trés Petit Corona	4½" x 35	

Strength Key: A = Mild, **B** = Mild to Medium, **C** = Medium, **D** = Medium to Strong, **E** = Strong

	SIZE	RATING
EL RICO HABANO		
USA & Dominican Republic C		
El Credito Cigars		
Corona	5¾" x 42	85
Double Corona	7" x 47	85
Gran Corona	5¾" x 46	89
Gran Habanero	7¾" x 50	
Gran Habanero Deluxe	7¾" x 50	80
Habano Club	5" x 48	90
Lonsdale Extra	6¼" x 44	
No. 1	7½" x 38	80
Petit Habano	5" x 40	89
EL SUBLIMADO		
Dominican Republic B		
Puros de Villa Gonzalez S.A.		
Churchill	8" x 50	85
Corona	6" x 44	84
Regardete	4½" x 50	85
Robusto	4½" x 50	87
Torpedo	7" x 54	86
ENCANTO		
Honduras C		
La Flor de Copan		
Cetros Natural Maduro		
Candella	6" x 42	
Churchill Maduro	6⅞" x 49	82
Corona Larga Natural	6½" x 44	
Elegante	7" x 44	86
Elegante Natural	7" x 43	
Grandotes Natural	7½" x 47	
Luchadores Natural		
Maduro	6¼" x 44	
Petit Corona Natural		
Maduro	5½" x 42	
Princessa Natural	4½" x 30	
Rothschild	4½" x 50	88
Rothschild Maduro	4½" x 50	85
Toro Maduro	6" x 50	86
Viajante Natural	8½" x 52	
EVELIO		
Honduras B		
Nestor Plasencia		
Corona	5¾" x 42	
Double Corona	7⅝" x 47	
No. 1	7" x 44	
Robusto	4¾" x 54	89
Robusto Larga	6" x 54	85
Torpedo	7" x 56	
EXCELSIOR		
Mexico B		
Nueva Matacan Tabacos S.A. de C.V.		
Individuale	8½" x 52	
No. 1	6¼" x 42	

	SIZE	RATING
No. 2	6¾" x 42	
No. 3	5½" x 52	81
No. 4	7" x 48	
No. 5	8" x 50	
F.D. GRAVE		
Honduras C		
Honduras Cuban Tobaccos		
Churchill	7¾" x 50	86
Corona Grande	7" x 52	
Lonsdale	6½" x 44	84
FELIPE GREGORIO		
Honduras C		
Cigars of Honduras		
Belicoso	6⅛" x 54	
Glorioso	7¾" x 50	
Nino	4¼" x 44	
Robusto	5" x 52	84
Sereno	5¾" x 42	86
Suntouso	7" x 48	
FIGHTING COCK		
Philippines C		
La Flor de la Isabella, Inc.		
C.O.D.	7" x 47	
Rooster Arturo	5" x 50	
Sidewinder	6" x 52	
Smokin' Lulu	5¼" x 48	
Texas Red	6½" x 50	
FLOR DE MANILA		
Philippines C		
Tabacalera de Philippines		
Cetros	6" x 39	
Cetros Largos	7½" x 39	
Churchill	7" x 47	
Corona	5½" x 44	
Coronas Largas	7" x 44	
Cortados	6" x tapered	
Londres	5¼" x 44	
Panatela	5" x 35	
FONSECA		
Cuba C		
Cosacos	5¼" x 42	81
Delicias	5¼" x 40	
Invictos	5¼" x 45	
K.D.T. Cadetes	6⅛" x 36	
No. 1	6⅓" x 44	
FONSECA		
Dominican Republic C/D		
Manufactura de Tabacos S.A. de C.V.		
2-2	4½" x 40	89
2-2 Maduro	4¼" x 40	
5-50	5" x 50	85

	SIZE	RATING
5-50 Maduro	5" x 50	
500	5½" x 43	
7-9-9	6½" x 46	
7-9-9 Maduro	6½" x 46	
700	6" x 50	
8-9-8	6" x 43	**88**
10-10	7" x 50	**86**
10-10 Maduro	6¾" x 49	**85**
No. 2	6¼" x 38	
Triangulare	5½" x 56	**87**

FUENTE FUENTE OPUS X
***Dominican Republic* E**
Tabacalera A. Fuente y Cia.

Double Corona	7⅝" x 49	**93**
Fuente Fuente	5⅝" x 46	**91**
Number 2	6¼" x 52	**92**
Perfecxion No. 2	6⅛" x 52	
Perfecxion No. 5	4⅞" x 40	
Petit Lancero	6" x 38	**91**
Reserva d' Chateau	7" x 48	
Robusto	5¼" x 50	**91**

GILBERTO OLIVA
***Honduras* C**
Nestor Plasencia

Churchill	7" x 50	
Churchill Maduro	7" x 50	
Numero 1	6½" x 44	**83**
Robusto	5" x 50	**85**
Robusto Maduro	5" x 50	
Torpedo	6½" x 52	
Viajante	6" x 52	**86**

GISPERT
***Cuba* B**

Coronas	5½" x 42	
Pt. Coronas De Luxe	5" x 42	

GISPERT
***Honduras* B**
Nestor Plasencia

Churchill	7½" x 50	
Lonsdale	6½" x 44	
Robusto	5" x 52	
Toro	6" x 50	

H. UPMANN
***Cuba* D**

	SIZE	RATING
Amatista	5¾" x 40	
Cinco Bocas	6½" x 42	
Connossieur No. 1	5" x 48	
Corona	5½" x 42	**91**
Corona Major	5⅛" x 42	
Corona Minor	4½" x 40	
Cristales	5¼" x 42	
Grand Corona	5¾" x 40	
Lonsdale	6½" x 42	**90**
Magnum	5½" x 46	**83**
Magnum 46	5⅝" x 46	
Medias Coronas	5" x 42	
Monarca	7" x 47	
No. 4 Alfred Dunhill	6½" x 46	**95**
No. 22 Alfred Dunhill Seleccion Suprema	4½" x 55	**94**
Noellas	5¼" x 42	
Petit Corona	5" x 42	**81**
Petit Palatinos	4½" x 36	
Royal Coronas	5½" x 42	
Short Coronas	5¼" x 42	
Sir Winston	7" x 47	
Super Coronas	5⅝" x 46	
Upmann No. 1	6½" x 42	
Upmann No. 2	6⅛" x 52	**89**
Upmann No. 4	5" x 42	

H. UPMANN
***Dominican Republic* C**
Consolidated Cigar Corp.

Amatista	5⅞" x 41	
Apéritif	4" x 28	
Churchill	5¾" x 46	**87**
Colombos	8" x 50	
Columbos 10's	8" x 50	
Corona	5⅝" x 42	**86**
Corona Brava	6½" x 48	
Corona Cristal	5 9/16" x 42	
Corona Imperial	7" x 46	
Corona Major	5⅛" x 42	**83**
Corona Major Tube	5 1/16" x 42	**85**
Corsario	5½" x 50	**86**
Demi Tasse	4½" x 33	
Director Royale	6⅝" x 42	**85**
El Prado	7" x 36	
Emperadores	7¾" x 46	
Extra Finos Tube	6¾" x 36	
Finos Tube	6¾" x 36	
Lonsdale	6⅝" x 42	**83**
Monarch	7" x 47	**84**
Naturales	6⅛" x 36	**83**
Panatela Cristal	6¾" x 38	
Pequeño 100	4½" x 50	**86**
Pequeño 200	4½" x 46	
Pequeño 300	4½" x 42	
Petit Corona	5 1/16" x 42	**86**
Robusto	4¾" x 42	**86**
Topacio	5¼" x 43	
Tubos	5⅛" x 42	**86**
Tubos Gold Tube	5⅛" x 42	
2000	7" x 43	

Strength Key: A = Mild, **B** = Mild to Medium, **C** = Medium, **D** = Medium to Strong, **E** = Strong

	SIZE	RATING
H. UPMANN CHAIRMAN'S		
RESERVE		
Dominican Republic C		
Consolidated Cigar Corp.		
Chairman's Reserve	7½" x 38	
Churchill	6¾" x 48	
Double Corona	7" x 50	
Robusto	4¾" x 50	
Torpedo	6" x 50	
H.A. LADRILLO		
Honduras B		
La Flor de Copan		
Fabuloso (perfecto shape)	7" x 48	
Imperial	7½" x 52	
Lancero	6½" x 44	
Robusto	5" x 52	
HABANA GOLD		
Honduras B		
Flor de Honduras Tabacos S.A.		
Churchill Black Label	7½" x 46	84
Churchill White Label	7" x 52	85
Corona Black Label	6" x 44	86
Corona White Label	6" x 44	
Double Corona		
Black Label	7½" x 46	
Double Corona		
White Label	7½" x 46	
No. 2	6⅛" x 52	
Petit Corona Black Label	5" x 42	
Petit Corona White Label	5" x 42	
Presidente Black Label	8½" x 52	
Presidente White Label	8½" x 32	
Robusto Black Label	5" x 50	80
Robusto White Label	5" x 50	87
Super Finos	4" x 20	
Torpedo Black Label	6" x 52	85
Torpedo White Label	6" x 52	
HABANICA		
Nicaragua C		
Cigars of Honduras		
Serie 546	5¼" x 46	87
Serie 550	5" x 50	88
Serie 638	6" x 38	85
Serie 646	6" x 46	85
Serie 747	7" x 47	
HAMILTONS		
Dominican Republic C		
Consolidated Cigar Corp.		
George I	7½" x 48	
George II	5" x 50	
George III	6" x 50	
George IV	6½" x 44	

	SIZE	RATING
HAMILTONS RESERVE		
Dominican Republic B		
Tabacos Dominicanos S.A.		
King George	7½" x 50	
Robusto	5" x 50	
Torpedo	6⅛" x 52	
HAVANA CLASSICO		
U.S.A. & Dominican Republic B		
Caribbean Cigar Co.		
Churchill	7¼" x 50	
Connecticut Robusto	5" x 50	85
Corona Classico	6½" x 42	
Double Corona	7½" x 46	
Malecon	9" x 60	86
Presidente	7½" x 54	
Puntas	5" x 48	
Pyramid	7¼" x 54	
Robusto	5" x 50	86
Robusto Largo	6" x 50	85
Torpedo	6½" x 54	
Varadero	5½" x 44	
HENRY CLAY		
Dominican Republic C		
Consolidated Cigar Corp.		
Brevas	5⅛" x 42	84
Brevas a la Conserva	5⅝" x 46	78
Brevas Fina Maduro	6½" x 48	84
HOYO DE MONTERREY		
Cuba E		
Churchill	7" x 47	88
Concorde	7" x 47	
Corona	5½" x 42	85
Double Corona	7⅝" x 49	96
Epicure No. 1	5¾" x 46	92
Epicure No. 2	5" x 50	92
Hoyo Coronas	5½" x 42	
Jeanne D'Arc	5⅝" x 35	
Le Hoyo des Dieux	6" x 42	09
Le Hoyo du Dauphin	6" x 38	88
Le Hoyo du Député	4⅛" x 38	
Le Hoyo du Gourmet	6⅖" x 33	
Le Hoyo du Maire	4" x 30	
Le Hoyo du Prince	5" x 40	86
Le Hoyo du Roi	5½" x 42	90
Longos	7" x 33	
Margaritas	4¾" x 26	
Odeón	6" x 38	
Opera	5⅛" x 42	
Particulares	9¼" x 47	93
Short Hoyo Corona	5" x 42	
Versaille	6¾" x 33	

	SIZE	RATING
HOYO DE MONTERREY		
Honduras **C**		
Villazon & Co.		
Ambassador	6" x 44	84
Ambassador Maduro	6" x 44	
Cafe Royal	6" x 43	87
Churchill	6¼" x 45	86
Churchill Maduro	6¼" x 45	
Corona	5⅝" x 46	87
Corona Maduro	5⅝" x 46	
Cuban Largo	7½" x 47	
Cuban Largo Maduro	7½" x 47	
Culebra	6" x 35	84
Delights	6½" x 37	80
Demi Tasse	4" x 39	86
Double Corona	6¾" x 48	83
Double Corona Maduro	6¾" x 48	
Dreams	5¾" x 46	
Governor	6" x 48	87
Governor Maduro	6⅛" x 50	86
Largo Elegante	7" x 32	
Largo Elegante Maduro	7" x 32	
Margaritas	5¼" x 29	
No. 1	6½" x 43	85
No. 55	5¼" x 43	88
Petit	4½" x 32	
President	8½" x 52	
President Maduro	8½" x 52	
Rothschild	4½" x 50	86
Rothschild Maduro	4½" x 50	85
Sabrosos	5" x 40	70
Sabrosos Maduro	5" x 40	
Sultan	7" x 52	82
Sultan Maduro	7" x 52	85
Super Hoyo	5½" x 44	87

	SIZE	RATING
HOYO DE MONTERREY		
EXCALIBUR		
Honduras **D**		
Villazon & Co.		
Banquet Tube	6¾" x 48	82
Number I	7¼" x 54	80
Number I Maduro	7¼" x 54	85
Number II	6¾" x 47	85
Number II Maduro	6¾" x 47	
Number III	6⅛" x 48	89
Number III Maduro	6⅛" x 48	87
Number IV	5⅝" x 46	81
Number IV Maduro	5⅝" x 46	
Number V	6¼" x 45	85
Number V Maduro	6¼" x 45	
Number VI	5½" x 38	85
Number VI Maduro	5½" x 38	
Number VII	5" x 43	88

	SIZE	RATING
HUGO CASSAR		
Dominican Republic **A**		
Hugo Cassar		
Diamond Selection		
Corona	5½" x 42	
Diamond Selection		
El Presidente	8" x 50	
Diamond Selection		
Grand Corona	6" x 46	
Diamond Selection		
Lonsdale	7" x 44	
Diamond Selection		
Robusto	4¾" x 50	
Diamond Seletion Toro	6½" x 52	
Mystique Churchill	8" x 50	
Mystique Lonsdale	7" x 44	
Mystique Maestro	7" x 48	
Mystique Toro	6¼" x 50	
Mystique Torpedo	6" x 53	
Private Collection		
Presidente	7½" x 49	
Private Collection		
Robusto	5" x 50	
Private Collection Toro	6½" x 52	
Private Collection		
Torpedo	6" x 53	

	SIZE	RATING
HUGO CASSAR		
Honduras **A**		
Hugo Cassar		
Diamond Selection		
Chairman	7¾" x 50	
Diamond Selection		
Corona	5½" x 44	
Diamond Selection		
Double Corona	6¼" x 52	
Diamond Selection		
Lonsdale	6⅝" x 46	
Diamond Selection		
Presidente	7" x 49	
Diamond Selection		
Robusto	5" x 50	
Diamond Selection		
Torpedo	6" x 53	
Mystique Churchill	7¾" x 47	
Mystique Corona	6" x 44	
Mystique Toro	6½" x 52	
Mystique Torpedo	6" x 53	
Private Collection		
Elegantes	6" x 50	
Private Collection		
Emperador	7¾" x 47	
Private Collection		
Imperial	7" x 44	

Strength Key: A = Mild, **B** = Mild to Medium, **C** = Medium, **D** = Medium to Strong, **E** = Strong

	SIZE	RATING
Private Collection		
Matador	6" x 42	
Private Collection		
Robusto	4¾" x 52	
HUGO CASSAR		
Mexico **A**		
Hugo Cassar		
Private Collection		
Churchill	7½" x 50	
Private Collection		
Corona	6" x 42	
Private Collection		
Robusto	5½" x 52	
Private Collection		
Rothschild	4½" x 50	
Private Collection Toro	6½" x 50	
HUGO CASSAR		
Nicaragua **A**		
Hugo Cassar		
Signature Churchill	7" x 48	
Signature Corona	5½" x 42	
Signature Giant	8" x 54	
Signature Lonsdale	6¾" x 44	
Signature Robusto	4¾" x 52	
Signature Toro	6" x 50	
JOSÉ BENITO		
Dominican Republic **C**		
Manufactura de Tabacos S.A. de C.V.		
Chico	4¼" x 32	
Churchill	7" x 50	84
Corona	6¾" x 43	
Havanitos	5" x 50	
Magnum	8¾" x 60	
Palma	6" x 43	87
Panatela	6¾" x 38	83
Petite	5½" x 38	87
Presidente	7¾" x 50	85
Rothschild	4¾" x 50	84
JOSÉ L. PIEDRA		
Cuba **B**		
Superiores	5¼" x 40	
JOSÉ L. PIEDRA		
Nicaragua **B**		
Tabacos Centroamericanos S.A.		
Emperador	7½" x 50	
Excellentes	5" x 50	
Gran Presidente	6⅞" x 46	
Robusto	5½" x 52	

	SIZE	RATING
JOSÉ LLOPIS		
Panama **B**		
Panama Cigar Co. S.A.		
Churchill	7" x 48	
No. 1	7" x 43	
No. 2	6½" x 43	
No. 4	5½" x 43	
Rothschild	4½" x 50	
Viajante	8½" x 52	
JOSÉ MARTÍ		
Dominican Republic **A**		
Manufactura de Tabacos S.A. de C.V.		
Corona	5½" x 42	84
Créme	6" x 35	
Maceo	6⅞" x 45	81
Martí	7¼" x 50	86
Palma	7" x 42	84
Remedio	5½" x 45	85
Robusto	5½" x 50	88
JOSÉ MARTÍ		
Nicaragua **B**		
Nicaraguan American Tobaccos S.A.		
1853	4½" x 35	
1868	5⅝" x 45	89
1871	4½" x 50	
1878	6½" x 48	
1892	7½" x 50	
1895	6½" x 52	
JOYA DE NICARAGUA		
Nicaragua **C**		
Tabacos Puros de Nicaragua &		
Nestor Plasencia		
Churchill	6⅞" x 49	83
Consul	4½" x 52	90
Corona	5⅝" x 48	
#1	6⅞" x 44	82
#3	6" x 44	
#5	4¼" x 38	85
#6	6" x 42	83
Petite	5½" x 38	82
Presidente Maduro		
Deluxe	7½" x 50	84
Robusto Maduro Deluxe	4¾" x 52	88
Señorita	5½" x 34	
Toro	6" x 50	84
Toro Maduro Deluxe	6" x 50	
Viajante	8½" x 52	88
JUAN CLEMENTE		
Dominican Republic **B**		
Cia. Tabacalera Santiaguense		
"530"	5" x 30	86
Churchill	6⅞" x 46	88

179

	SIZE	RATING
Club Selection No. 1	6" x 50	83
Club Selection No. 2	4½" x 46	84
Club Selection No. 3	7" x 44	84
Club Selection No. 4	5¾" x 42	86
Club Selection Obelisco	6" x 54	
Corona	5" x 42	
Demi Corona	4" x 40	
Demi Tasse	3⅝" x 34	
Especiale	7½" x 38	
Especiale No. 2	6" x 38	
Gargantua	13" x 50	
Gigante	9" x 50	
Grand Corona	6" x 42	84
Mini	4⅛" x 22	
Panatela	6½" x 34	83
Rothschild	4⅞" x 50	85

JUAN LOPEZ
Cuba **D**

	SIZE	RATING
Coronas	5½" x 42	
Patricias	4½" x 40	
Petit Coronas	5" x 42	
Placeras	4⅞" x 34	
Selección No. 1	5½" x 46	
Selección No. 2	4¾" x 50	90

KNOCKANDO
Dominican Republic **B**
Tabacos Dominicanos S.A.

	SIZE	RATING
No. 3	5¾" x 41	84

LA AURORA
Dominican Republic **C**
La Aurora S.A.

	SIZE	RATING
Bristol Especiale	6⅜" x 48	84
Cetros	6⅜" x 41	
Corona	5" x 37	
Double Corona	7½" x 50	
No. 4	5¼" x 42	85
Palmas Extra	6¾" x 35	80
Petit Corona	4½" x 37	
Robusto	5" x 50	87
Sublimes	5" x 38	

LA CORONA
Dominican Republic **B**
Consolidated Cigar Corp.

	SIZE	RATING
Aristocrats	6⅛" x 36	
Corona Chicas	5½" x 42	
Directors	6½" x 46	

LA DILIGENCIA
Honduras **B**
Nestor Plasencia

	SIZE	RATING
Churchill	7" x 48	
Gran Corona	6" x 44	
Presidente	8½" x 52	

	SIZE	RATING
Robusto	4¾" x 50	
Toro	6" x 50	

LA DIVA
Dominican Republic **A**
Puros de Villa Gonzalez S.A.

	SIZE	RATING
Churchill	8" x 50	
Corona	6" x 44	
Robusto	4½" x 50	
Torpedo	7" x 54	

LA FINCA
Nicaragua **D**
Nestor Plasencia

	SIZE	RATING
Bolivar	7½" x 50	85
Corona	5½" x 42	84
Flora	7" x 36	86
Gran Finca	8½" x 52	
Joya	6" x 50	79
Pico	6" x 36	85
Robusto	4½" x 50	77
Romeo	6½" x 42	87

LA FLOR DOMINICANA
Dominican Republic **B**
La Flor Dominicana

	SIZE	RATING
Alcalde	6½" x 44	82
Belicosos	5½" x 52	
Churchill	6⅞" x 49	
Diplomaticos	5" x 30	87
Figurado	6½" x 52	
Insurrectos	5½" x 42	
Maceo	5" x 48	85
Macheteros	4" x 40	
Mambises	6⅞" x 48	
Robusto	5" x 48	
Robusto Reserva Especial	5" x 48	87

LA FLOR DE CANO
Cuba **C**

	SIZE	RATING
Corona	5" x 42	
Diademas	7" x 47	89
Gran Corona	5⅝" x 46	
Short Churchill	5" x 50	93

LA FLOR DE LA ISABELLA
Philippines **B**
La Flor de la Isabella, Inc.

	SIZE	RATING
Don Juan Urquijo Churchill	7" x 47	
Don Juan Urquijo Corona	5½" x 44	
Don Juan Urquijo Figurado	5½" x 42	
Don Juan Urquijo Panatela	4½" x 32	

Strength Key: A = Mild, **B** = Mild to Medium, **C** = Medium, **D** = Medium to Strong, **E** = Strong

	SIZE	RATING
Don Juan Urquijo		
Pyramid	6⅛" x 52	
Don Juan Urquijo		
Robusto	5" x 50	
Tabacara Corona Largas	6⅞" x 44	
Tabacara Coronas	5½" x 44	
Tabacara Coronas		
Largas Especiales	8" x 47	
Tabacara Double		
Corona	8½" x 50	
Tabacara Half Corona	3⅞" x 37	
Tabacara Panatela	4¾" x 35	
Tabacara Pyramid	6⅛" x 52	
Tabacara Robusto	5" x 50	

LA FONTANA
Honduras   A
Caribe Imported Cigars Inc.

	SIZE	RATING
Belicoso	6" x 54	
Da Vinci	6⅞" x 48	84
Dante	5½" x 38	
Galileo	5" x 50	
Michelangelo	7½" x 52	83
Mona Lisa	4¾" x 46	
Puccini	6½" x 44	
Rossini	5½" x 33	
Verdi	5½" x 44	

LA GLORIA CUBANA
Cuba   D/E

Cetros	6½" x 42	
Medaille d'Or 1	7⅛" x 36	87
Medaille d'Or 2	6⅔" x 43	90
Medaille d'Or 3	7" x 28	
Medaille d'Or 4	6" x 32	84
Minutos	4½" x 40	
Sabrosos	6¼" x 42	
Tapados	5¼" x 42	
Taínos	7" x 47	

LA GLORIA CUBANA
U.S.A. & Dominican Republic   D/E
El Credito Cigars

Charlemagne	7¼" x 54	
Charlemagne Maduro	7¼" x 54	
Churchill	7" x 50	89
Churchill Maduro	7" x 50	
Corona	6" x 52	
Corona Extra Larga	7¾" x 44	
Corona Extra Larga		
Maduro	7¾" x 44	
Corona Gorda	6" x 52	
Corona Gorda Maduro	6" x 52	
Crown Imperial	9" x 49	
Double Corona	7¾" x 49	
Double Corona Maduro	7¾" x 49	
Glorias	5½" x 43	88

	SIZE	RATING
Glorias Maduro	5½" x 43	
Glorias Extra	6¼" x 46	87
Glorias Extra Maduro	6¼" x 46	
Inmensas	7½" x 48	
Inmensas Maduro	7½" x 48	
Medaille d'Or No. 1	6¾" x 43	88
Medaille d'Or No. 1		
Maduro	6¾" x 43	
Medaille d'Or No. 2	6¼" x 43	
Medaille d'Or No. 2		
Maduro	6¼" x 43	
Medaille d'Or No. 3	7" x 28	
Medaille d'Or No. 4	6" x 32	
Minutos	4" x 40	
Panatela Deluxe	7" x 37	87
Panatela Deluxe Maduro	7" x 37	
Pyramid	7¼" x 56	
Pyramid Maduro	7½" x 56	
Soberano	8" x 52	91
Soberano Maduro	8" x 52	
Torpedo No. 1	6½"	86
Torpedo No. 1 Maduro	6½"	86
Wavell	5" x 50	85
Wavell Maduro	5" x 50	90

LA HABANERA
Dominican Republic   B
Tabacalera A. Fuente y Cia.

Churchills	6⅞" x 46	
Diplomaticos	6" x 44	
Elegantes	6¾" x 42	
Emperadores	5½" x 50	
Especiales	5" x 30	
Presidents	7½" x 50	
Puritanos	5¾" x 42	
Selectos	7" x 36	

LA HOJA SELECTA
U.S.A. & Dominican Republic   B
El Credito Cigars

Bel Aires	6¾" x 38	
Cetros de Oro	5¾" x 43	83
Chateau Sovereign	7½" x 52	
Choix Supreme	7" x 48	
Cosiac	7" x 48	85
Geneves	6½" x 32	
Palais Royal	4¾" x 50	72
Selectos No. 1	6½" x 42	
Selectos de Lujo	7" x 45	

LA PLATA
U.S.A.   B
La Plata Cigar Co.

Enterprise Classic	7" x 52	
Grand Classic	6" x 44	
Hercules	5½" x 54	
Magnificos Maduro	6" x 44	

	SIZE	RATING
Robusto Uno Maduro	4½" x 52	
Royal Wilshire Maduro	7" x 52	

LA REGENTA
Canary Islands **B**
La Regenta

	SIZE	RATING
Especial 1923 No. 2	4¾" x 50	
Gran Corona	7¼" x 46	
Individual	8" x 50	
No. 1	6¾" x 42	**78**
No. 3	5¾" x 42	
No. 4	5⅛" x 42	
No. 5	4½" x 42	
Pyramid	7" x 36/52	
Premier	7½" x 50	
Robusto	4¾" x 50	**83**

LA RESERVA
Honduras **C**
Tabacos de Oriente

	SIZE	RATING
No. 2	6½" x 48	**86**

LA TRADICION
U.S.A. **C**
Nick's Cigar Co.

	SIZE	RATING
Cabinet Series Natural Robusto	5" x 50	**78**
Cabinet Series Rosado Robusto	5" x 50	**81**
Churchill	7" x 44	
Corona	6" x 44	
Double Corona	7⅝" x 50	
Gran Torpedo	7½" x 60	
Torpedo	6½" x 54	

LA UNICA
Dominican Republic **C**
Tabacalera A. Fuente y Cia.

	SIZE	RATING
No. 100	8½" x 52	**90**
No. 200	7" x 49	**88**
No. 200 Maduro	7" x 49	**86**
No. 300	6¾" x 44	**84**
No. 400	4½" x 50	**88**
No. 400 Maduro	4½" x 50	**84**
No. 500	5½" x 42	**84**

LAS CABRILLAS
Honduras **C**
Consolidated Cigar Corp.

	SIZE	RATING
Balboa	7½" x 54	**82**
Balboa Maduro	7½" x 54	**82**
Columbus	8¼" x 52	
Columbus Maduro	8¼" x 52	
Coronado	6⅞" x 35	
Cortez	4¾" x 50	**83**
Cortez Maduro	4¾" x 50	**84**
De Soto	6⅞" x 50	**83**
De Soto Maduro	6⅞" x 50	
Magellan	6" x 42	**84**
Maximillian	7" x 55	**84**
Maximillian Maduro	7" x 56	
Pizarro	5½" x 32	**85**
Ponce de Leon	6⅝" x 44	**79**
Ponce de Leon Maduro	6⅝" x 44	

LEMPIRA
Honduras **B**
Nestor Plasencia

	SIZE	RATING
Churchill	7" x 48	**86**
Corona	5½" x 42	**88**
Lancero	7½" x 38	
Lonsdale	6½" x 44	
Presidente	7¾" x 50	
Robusto	5" x 50	**80**
Toro	6" x 50	**89**

LEON JIMENES
Dominican Republic **C**
La Aurora S.A.

	SIZE	RATING
No. 1	7½" x 50	**83**
No. 2	7" x 47	**86**
No. 3	6½" x 42	**83**
No. 4	5 9/16" x 42	**85**
No. 5	5" x 38	
Robusto	5½" x 50	**88**
Torpedo	6½" x 52	

LICENCIADOS
Dominican Republic **D**
Manufactura de Tabacos S.A. de C.V.

	SIZE	RATING
Churchill	7" x 50	
Excelente	6¾" x 43	**87**
Expreso	4½" x 35	
Figurado	6" x 56	
Numero 4	5¾" x 43	**80**
Numero 4 Maduro	5¾" x 43	**86**
Panatela Lindas	7" x 38	**82**
Presidentes	8" x 50	**80**
Soberanos	8½" x 52	
Supreme Maduro No. 200	5¾" x 43	**82**
Supreme Maduro No. 300	6¾" x 43	
Supreme Maduro No. 400	6" x 50	**84**
Supreme Maduro No. 500	8" x 50	
Toro	6" x 50	**86**
Wavell	5" x 50	**86**
Wavell Maduro	5" x 50	**87**

Strength Key: A = Mild, **B** = Mild to Medium, **C** = Medium, **D** = Medium to Strong, **E** = Strong

MACABI

Dominican Republic C/D

Tabacalera A. Fuente y Cia.

	SIZE	RATING
Belicoso Fino	6¼" x 52	88
Corona Extra	6" x 50	84
Double Corona	6⅞" x 49	
Media Corona	5½" x 43	86
No. 1	6¾" x 44	85
Royal Corona	5" x 50	84
Super Corona	7¾" x 52	

MACANUDO

Jamaica & Dominican Republic B/C

General Cigar Co.

	SIZE	RATING
Amatista	6¼" x 42	89
Ascot	4¼" x 32	
Baron de Rothschild	6½" x 42	85
Baron de Rothschild Maduro	6½" x 42	
Caviar	4" x 36	
Claybourne	6" x 31	83
Crystal	5½" x 50	85
Crystal Cafe	5½" x 50	84
Crystal Tube	5½" x 50	84
Duke of Devon	5½" x 42	86
Duke of Devon Maduro	5½" x 42	83
Duke of Wellington	8½" x 38	86
Duke of Windsor	6" x 50	87
Hampton Court	5¾" x 43	85
Hyde Park	5½" x 49	85
Hyde Park Maduro	5½" x 49	88
Lord Claridge	5½" x 38	88
Petit Corona	5" x 38	84
Portofino	7" x 34	85
Prince Philip	7½" x 49	85
Prince Philip Maduro	7½" x 49	85
Prince of Wales Cafe	8" x 52	
Vintage Cabinet I	7½" x 49	90
Vintage Cabinet II	6⁹⁄₁₆" x 43	86
Vintage Cabinet III	5⁹⁄₁₆" x 43	86
Vintage Cabinet IV	4½" x 47	
Vintage Cabinet V	5½" x 49	85
Vintage Cabinet VII	7½" x 38	83
Vintage Cabinet VIII Crystal	5½" x 50	84

MACANUDO VINTAGE 1993

Jamaica B

General Cigar Co.

	SIZE	RATING
No. I	7½" x 49	
No. II	6⁹⁄₁₆" x 43	
No. III	5⁹⁄₁₆" x 43	
No. IV	4½" x 47	87
No. V	5½" x 49	88
No. VIII	5½" x 50	90

MARIO PALOMINO

Jamaica B

Palomino

	SIZE	RATING
Buccaneers	5½" x 32	
Caballero	7" x 45	
Cetro	6½" x 42	
Corona Inmensa	6" x 47	
Delicado	5½" x 32	
Festivale	6" x 41	
Petit Corona	5" x 41	
Presidente	7½" x 49	
Rapier	6" x 32	

MATACAN

Mexico C

Nueva Matacan Tabacos S.A. de C.V.

	SIZE	RATING
Natural	4¾" x 50	
Maduro	4¾" x 50	
Natural	6⅝" x 46	
Maduro	6⅝" x 46	
Natural	6⅞" x 54	
Maduro	6⅞" x 54	
Natural	6" x 50	
Maduro	6" x 50	
Natural	7½" x 40	
Maduro	7½" x 40	

MATCH PLAY

Dominican Republic B

Tabacos Dominicanos S.A.

	SIZE	RATING
Cypress	4¾" x 50	84
Olympic	7½" x 50	
Prestwick	6⅞" x 46	
St. Andrews	6¼" x 44	
Troon	7" x 54	
Turnberry	6" x 50	80

MAYA

Honduras B

Nestor Plasencia

	SIZE	RATING
Cetros	6" x 43	
Cetros Maduro	6" x 43	
Churchill	6⅞" x 49	85
Churchill Maduro	6⅞" x 49	
Corona	6¼" x 44	
Coronas Maduro	6¼" x 44	
Elegante	7" x 43	
Executive	7¾" x 50	
Executive Maduro	7¾" x 50	
Matador	6" x 50	83
Matador Maduro	6" x 50	
Palma Fina	6⅞" x 36	86
Petit	5½" x 34	82
Petit Corona	5½" x 42	85
Robusto	5" x 50	
Robusto Maduro	5" x 50	

	SIZE	RATING
Torpedo	7" x 54	
Viajantes	8½" x 52	
MI CUBANO		
Nicaragua **C**		
Nestor Plasencia		
No. 450	4" x 50	
No. 542	5" x 42	84
No. 644	6" x 44	
No. 650	6" x 50	82
No. 748	7" x 48	
No. 852	8" x 52	
MOCHA SUPREME		
Honduras **B**		
Nestor Plasencia		
Allegro	6½" x 36	
Baron Rothschild	4½" x 52	
Lord	6½" x 42	
Patroon	7½" x 50	
Petit	4½" x 42	
Rembrandt	8½" x 52	
Renaissance	6" x 50	
Sovereign	5½" x 42	
MONTE CANARIO		
Canary Islands **B**		
Tayco Trading SL		
Imperiales	6½" x 42	86
#3	5¾" x 42	
Nuncio	6¾" x 44	86
Panatela	6" x 38	80
Robusto	4¾" x 50	70
MONTECRISTO		
Cuba **C/D**		
"A"	9½" x 47	91
Especial	7½" x 38	86
Especial No. 1	7½" x 38	91
Especial No. 2	6" x 38	87
Joyitas	4½" x 26	
No. 1	6½" x 42	88
No. 2	6" x 52	94
No. 3	5½" x 42	88
No. 4	5" x 42	89
No. 5	4" x 40	
No. 6	4⅞" x 33	
No. 7	7" x 28	
Tubos	6⅛" x 42	
MONTECRISTO		
Dominican Republic **D**		
Consolidated Cigar Corp.		
Churchill	7" x 48	89
Corona Grande	5¾" x 46	86
Double Corona	6¼" x 50	86

	SIZE	RATING
No. 1	6½" x 44	87
No. 2	6" x 50	87
No. 3	5½" x 44	87
Robusto	4¾" x 50	89
Tubos	6¼" x 42	
MONTECRUZ		
Dominican Republic **C**		
Consolidated Cigar Corp.		
Junior	5¼" x 33	
Robusto	4½" x 49	88
Señores	5¾" x 35	
Sun-Grown Cedar Aged	5" x 42	83
Sun-Grown Colossus	6½" x 50	
Sun-Grown Individuales	8" x 46	84
Sun-Grown No. 200	7¼" x 46	88
Sun-Grown No. 201	6¼" x 46	85
Sun-Grown No. 205	7" x 42	
Sun-Grown No. 210	6½" x 42	84
Sun-Grown No. 220	5½" x 42	87
Sun-Grown No. 230	5" x 42	84
Sun-Grown No. 250	6½" x 38	
Sun-Grown No. 255	7" x 36	
Sun-Grown No. 265	5½" x 38	
Sun-Grown No. 270	4¾" x 36	
Sun-Grown No. 276	6" x 32	85
Sun-Grown No. 280	7" x 28	
Sun-Grown No. 281	6" x 28	80
Sun-Grown No. 282	5" x 28	
Sun-Grown Robusto	4½" x 49	83
Sun-Grown Tubos	6" x 42	85
Sun-Grown Tubulares	6⅛" x 38	84
MONTERO		
Dominican Republic **B**		
Tabacos Dominicanos S.A.		
Cetro	6" x 44	
Churchill	6⅞" x 46	
Presidente	7½" x 50	
Robusto	6" x 50	
Toro	6" x 50	
Torpedo	7" x 35	
MONTESINO		
Dominican Republic **C**		
Tabacalera A. Fuente y Cia.		
Cesar No. 2	6¼" x 44	83
Diplomatico	5½" x 42	91
Diplomatico Maduro	5½" x 42	86
Fumas	6¾" x 44	
Gran Corona	6¾" x 48	86
Gran Corona Maduro	6¾" x 48	86
Napoleon Grande	7" x 46	
Napoleon Grande Maduro	7½" x 46	
No. 1	6¾" x 43	87
No. 1 Maduro	6⅞" x 43	

	SIZE	RATING
No. 2	6¼" x 44	
No. 2 Maduro	6¼" x 44	
No. 3	6¾" x 36	
No. 3 Maduro	6¾" x 36	

Moreno Maduro

Dominican Republic **B**

Manufactura de Tabacos S.A. de C.V.

#326	6" x 32	
#426	6½" x 42	
#445	5½" x 44	
#467	7" x 46	
#486	6" x 48	
#507	7" x 50	
#528	8½" x 52	

Nat Sherman

Dominican Republic C

Consolidated Cigar Corp. & General Cigar Co.

	SIZE	RATING
Academy #2	5" x 31	
Algonquin	6¾" x 43	**84**
Butterfield #8	6½" x 42	**83**
City Desk Dispatch	6½" x 46	**85**
City Desk Gazette	6" x 42	**83**
City Desk Telegraph Maduro	6" x 50	**85**
City Desk Tribune	7½" x 50	**86**
Exchange Selection Academy No. 2	5" x 31	**78**
Exchange Selection Butterfield #8	6½" x 42	**83**
Exchange Selection Murray Hill #7	6" x 38	**85**
Exchange Selection Oxford #5	7" x 49	**88**
Exchange Selection Trafalgar #4	6" x 47	**82**
Gotham Selection #65	6" x 32	**84**
Gotham Selection #500	7" x 50	**87**
Gotham Selection #711	6" x 50	**87**
Gotham Selection #1400	6¼" x 44	**85**
Landmark Selection Algonquin	6¾" x 44	**85**
Landmark Selection Dakota	7½" x 49	**87**
Landmark Selection Hampshire	5½" x 42	**87**
Landmark Selection Metropole	6" x 34	**82**
Landmark Selection Vanderbilt	5" x 47	**82**
Manhattan Selection Beekman	5½" x 28	**79**
Manhattan Selection Chelsea	6½" x 38	**84**
Manhattan Selection Gramercy	6¾" x 43	**80**
Manhattan Selection Sutton	5½" x 49	**84**
Manhattan Selection Tribeca	6" x 31	**81**
Metropolitan Selection Angler	5½" x 43	**87**
Metropolitan Selection Metropolitan	7" x 52	**87**
Morgan	7" x 42	**80**
Murray Hill #3	6" x 38	
Murray Hill #7	6" x 38	**83**
Oxford	7" x 49	
Sutton	5½" x 49	**84**
Trafalgar No. 4	6" x 47	**84**
Tribune	7½" x 50	**86**
VIP Selection Astor	4½" x 50	**86**
VIP Selection Barnum Glass Tube	5½" x 42	**82**
VIP Selection Carnegie	6" x 48	**86**
VIP Selection Morgan	7" x 42	
VIP Selection Ziegfeld	6¾" x 38	**83**

Nat Sherman

Honduras C

Caribe Imported Cigars Inc.

Churchill	7½" x 50	
Corona	5½" x 42	
Hobart	5" x 50	**86**
Host Selection Hamilton	5½" x 42	**80**
Host Selection Hampton	7" x 50	
Host Selection Harrington	7" x 44	
Host Selection Hobart	5" x 50	**86**
Host Selection Hudson	5" x 32	
Host Selection Hunter	6½" x 43	
Imperial	8½" x 52	
Lonsdale	6½" x 42	
Royal Palm	6⅞" x 37	
Soberanos	6⅞" x 46	
Super Rothschild	6" x 50	

Nestor 747

Honduras C

Nestor Plasencia

Nestor 747	7⅝" x 47	
Cabinet Series No. 2 Robusto	4¾" x 54	**85**

Nestor 747 Vintage

Honduras C

Nestor Plasencia

454	4¾" x 54	
454 Maduro	4¾" x 54	
654	6" x 54	
747	7⅝" x 47	

	SIZE	RATING
Robusto	4¾" x 54	
Robusto Larga	6" x 54	
Robusto Maduro	4¾" x 54	

OLOR
Dominican Republic   **B**
Tabacalera A. Fuente y Cia.

	SIZE	RATING
Colossos	7½" x 48	88
Lonsdale	6½" x 42	84
Momentos	5½" x 43	88
Paco	6" x 50	88

ONYX
Dominican Republic   **B**
Consolidated Cigar Corp.

	SIZE	RATING
Number 642	6" x 42	83
Number 642 Maduro	6" x 42	85
Number 646	6⅝" x 46	85
Number 650	6" x 50	87
Number 650 Maduro	6" x 50	80
Number 750	7½" x 50	85
Number 750 Maduro	7½" x 50	85
Number 852	8" x 52	
Number 852 Maduro	8" x 52	

ORIENT EXPRESS
Honduras   **C**
Puros de Villa Gonzalez S.A.

	SIZE	RATING
Expresso	6" x 48	82
Le Club	7¾" x 50	
Le Twist #1	6" x 40	
Le Twist #2	8" x 38	
#2406	5" x 50	
#2407	6⅞" x 36	
#2410	6⅞" x 49	
#2414	4" x 40	
#2415	5½" x 44	
#2418	6⅝" x 44	

ORNELAS
Mexico   **B**
Tabacos Ornelas S.A.

	SIZE	RATING
Cafetero Chico	5½" x 46	
Cafetero Chico Maduro	5½" x 46	79
Cafetero Grande	6½" x 46	85
Churchill	7" x 49	79
Churchill Maduro	7" x 49	84
LTD 5 Al Cognac	6¼" x 42	
LTD 10 Al Cognac	6¼" x 42	
LTD 20 Al Cognac	6¼" x 42	
LTD 25 Al Cognac	6¼" x 42	
LTD 40 AL Cognac	6¼" x 42	
Matinee	6" x 30	85
Matinee Light	4¾" x 30	
#1	6¾" x 44	78
#1 Vanilla	6¾" x 44	69
#2	6" x 42	

	SIZE	RATING
#3	7" x 38	
#4	5" x 44	
#5	6" x 38	80
#5 Vanilla	6" x 38	
#6	5" x 38	81
#6 Vanilla	5" x 38	
#250	9½" x 64	87
Robusto	4¾" x 49	75
Robusto Maduro	4¾" x 49	86

OSCAR
Dominican Republic   **C**
Dominican Cigar C.A.

	SIZE	RATING
No. 300	6¼" x 44	81
No. 500	5½" x 50	81
No. 700	7" x 54	88
Supreme	8" x 48	88

PADRÓN
Honduras & Nicaragua   **C**
Tabacos Centroamericanos S.A.

	SIZE	RATING
2000	5" x 50	86
2000 Maduro	5" x 50	86
3000	5½" x 52	87
3000 Maduro	5½" x 52	88
Ambassador	6⅞" x 42	83
Chicos	5½" x 36	83
Churchill Maduro	6⅞" x 46	86
Delicias	4⅞" x 46	
Executive Maduro	7½" x 50	87
Grand Reserve	8" x 41	
Londres	5½" x 42	85
Magnum	9" x 50	91
Palmas	6⁵⁄₁₆" x 42	87
Panatela	6⅞" x 36	

PADRÓN 1964 ANNIVERSARY SERIES
Honduras & Nicaragua   **C**
Tabacos Centroamericanos S.A.

	SIZE	RATING
Corona	6" x 42	88
Diplomatico	7" x 50	
Exclusivo	5½" x 50	92
Monarca	6½" x 46	
Piramide	6⅞" x 52	82
Piramide Maduro	6⅞" x 52	
Superior	6½" x 42	83

PARTAGAS
Cuba   **D/E**

	SIZE	RATING
Astoria	5¼" x 42	
Charlotte	5⅝" x 35	
Churchill Deluxe	7" x 47	
Corona	5½" x 42	86
Coronas Grandes	6⅛" x 42	
Culebras	5¾" x 39	87
8-9-8	6⅛" x 43	88
Filipos	5¼" x 34	

Strength Key: A = Mild, **B** = Mild to Medium, **C** = Medium, **D** = Medium to Strong, **E** = Strong

	Size	Rating
Lonsdales	6½" x 42	
Lusitania	7⅝" x 49	**92**
No. 1	6⅝" x 43	**88**
No. 6 Selección Superba	4½" x 40	**93**
Palmas Grandes	7" x 33	
Partagas de Partagas	6⅔" x 43	
Petit Corona	5" x 42	**89**
Presidente	6" x 47	**84**
Ramonitas	4¾" x 26	
Royales	4⅞" x 40	
Selección Privada No. 1	6⅔" x 43	
Serie D No. 4	5" x 50	**92**
Short	4⅓" x 42	
Trés Petit Corona	4½" x 40	

PARTAGAS
Dominican Republic **D**
General Cigar Co.

	Size	Rating
Almirante	6" x 49	**85**
Aristocrat	6" x 50	
8-9-8	6⅞" x 44	**88**
Humitube	6¾" x 43	**87**
Limited Reserve Epicure	5" x 38	
Limited Reserve Regale	6¼" x 47	**87**
Limited Reserve Robusto	5½" x 49	
Limited Reserve Royale	6¾" x 43	**87**
Maduro	6¼" x 48	**85**
Naturales	5½" x 49	**83**
No. 1	6¾" x 43	**88**
No. 2	5⅞" x 44	**86**
No. 3	5¼" x 43	
No. 4	5" x 38	**84**
No. 6	6" x 34	**81**
No. 10	7½" x 49	**89**
Purito	4¼" x 32	
Robusto	4½" x 49	**87**
Sabroso	5⅞" x 44	**86**
Tubos	7" x 38	**82**

PARTICULARES
Honduras **B**
Tabacalera Universal

	Size	Rating
Churchill	6⅞" x 49	
Executive Pack	8½" x 52	
Matador	6" x 50	
Numero Cuatro	5½" x 42	
Panatelas	6⅞" x 35	
Petit	5⅝" x 34	**80**
Presidente	7¾" x 50	
Rothschild	5" x 50	
Royal Coronas	6¼" x 43	
Supremos	7" x 43	
Viajante	8½" x 52	

PAUL GARMIRIAN
Dominican Republic **D**
Tabacos Dominicanos S.A.

	Size	Rating
Belicoso	6¼" x 52	**88**
Belicoso Fino	5½" x 52	**86**
Bombone	3½" x 43	**87**
Celebration	9" x 50	**88**
Churchill	7" x 48	**82**
Connoisseur	6" x 50	**86**
Corona	5½" x 42	**86**
Corona Grande	6½" x 46	
Epicure	5½" x 50	**82**
Gourmet Double Corona	7⅝" x 50	**88**
Lonsdale	6½" x 42	**78**
No. 1	7½" x 38	
No. 2	4¾" x 48	**80**
No. 5	4" x 40	
P.G. Especial	5¾" x 38	
P.G. Reserve Gourmet	7⅝" x 50	**89**
Panatela	7½" x 38	**87**
Petit Bouquet	4½" x 38	
Petit Corona	5" x 43	**86**
Robusto	5" x 50	**81**

PENAMIL
Canary Islands **C**
Citas Tabacos de Canarias S.A.

	Size	Rating
No. 5	5⅓" x 41	
No. 6	5⅞" x 41	
No. 16	7⅛" x 38	
No. 17	6⅔" x 41	
No. 18	7⅛" x 44	
No. 25	7½" x 45	
No. 30	7⅔" x 45	
No. 50	6" x 50	
No. 57	7½" x 50	**69**

PETER STOKKEBYE
Dominican Republic **B**
Manufactura de Tabacos S.A. de C.V.

	Size	Rating
Santa Maria #1	7" x 50	
Santa Maria #2	6¾" x 38	
Santa Maria #3	5½" x 43	

PETERSON
Dominican Republic **B**
Cuervo y Hermano

	Size	Rating
Churchill	7" x 48	
Corona	5¾" x 43	**82**
Petit Corona	5" x 43	
Presidente	7½" x 50	
Robusto	4¾" x 50	**81**
Toro	6" x 50	**87**
Très Petite	4½" x 38	

	SIZE	RATING
PETRUS		
Honduras **C**		
Cigars of Honduras		
Antonius	5" x 54	86
Chantaco	4¾" x 35	
Churchill	7" x 50	82
Corona Sublime	6" x 50	85
DC Havana	7¾" x 50	86
Double Corona	7¾" x 50	87
Duchess	4½" x 30	
Gregorius	5" x 42	
Lord Byron	8" x 38	
No. II	6¼" x 44	
No. II Maduro	6¼" x 44	84
No. III	6" x 50	
No. IV	5⅝" x 38	
Palma Fina	6" x 38	82
Rothschild	4¾" x 50	74
Tabaccage 89 Antonius	5" x 20	
Tabaccage 89 Chantaco	4¾" x 35	
Tabaccage 89 Churchill	7" x 50	84
Tabaccage 89 Corona Sublime	5½" x 46	82
Tabaccage 89 Corona Sublime Maduro	5½" x 46	78
Tabaccage 89 Sublime Sublime Maduro	5½" x 46	72
Tabaccage 89 Double Corona	7¾" x 50	
Tabaccage 89 Duchess	4½" x 30	
Tabaccage 89 Gregorius	5" x 42	
Tabaccage 89 II	6¼" x 44	86
Tabaccage 89 III	6" x 50	
Tabaccage 89 IV	5⅝" x 38	83
Tabaccage 89 Lord Byron	8" x 38	
Tabaccage 89 Palma Fina	6½" x 25	
Tabaccage 89 Petrushkas	4¼" x 25	
Tabaccage 89 Rothschild	4¾" x 50	81
PLASENCIA		
Honduras **C**		
Nestor Plasencia		
#1 Maduro	7" x 43	
#1 Natural	7" x 43	
#3 Natural	7" x 36	
#4 Natural	5½" x 43	
#5 Natural	5½" x 35	
Churchill Maduro	7" x 49	
Churchill Natural	7" x 49	
Corona Especial Maduro	6" x 44	
Corona Especial Natural	6" x 44	
Gigante Maduro	8" x 54	
Gigante Natural	8" x 54	
Imperial Maduro	7½" x 50	
Imperial Natural	7½" x 50	
Rothschild Maduro	4½" x 50	
Rothschild Natural	4½" x 50	

	SIZE	RATING
Toro Maduro	6" x 50	
Toro Natural	6" x 50	
Torpedo Maduro	7" x 54	
Torpedo Natural	7" x 54	
Viajante Maduro	8½" x 52	
Viajante Natural	8½" x 52	
PLAYBOY BY DON DIEGO		
Dominican Republic **C**		
Consolidated Cigar Corp.		
Churchill	7¾" x 50	
Double Corona	6" x 52	
Gran Corona	6¾" x 48	
Lonsdale	6½" x 42	
Robusto	5" x 50	86
PLEIADES		
Dominican Republic **C**		
Manufactura de Tabacos S.A. de C.V.		
Aldebaran	8½" x 50	85
Antares	5½" x 40	82
Mars	5" x 28	82
Neptune	7½" x 42	79
Orion	5¾" x 42	81
Perseus	5" x 34	79
Pluton	5" x 50	83
Saturn	8" x 46	81
Sirius	6⅞" x 46	81
Uranus	6⅞" x 34	
POR LARRAÑAGA		
Cuba **B/C**		
Coronas	5½" x 42	
Coronitas	4⅜" x 34	
Lonsdale	6½" x 42	
Petit Corona	5" x 42	
Small Corona	4½" x 40	
POR LARRAÑAGA		
Dominican Republic **C**		
Consolidated Cigar Corp.		
Cetros	6⅞" x 42	87
Delicados	6½" x 36	82
Fabuloso	7" x 50	88
Nacionales	5½" x 42	84
Petit Cetros en Cedro	5" x 38	86
Pyramid	6" x 50	86
Robusto	5" x 50	87
PRIMO DEL REY		
Dominican Republic **C**		
Consolidated Cigar Corp.		
Aguilas	8" x 52	
Almirante	6" x 50	83
Almirante Maduro	6" x 50	85
Aristocrat	6¾" x 48	81
Barons	8½" x 52	

Strength Key: A = Mild, **B** = Mild to Medium, **C** = Medium, **D** = Medium to Strong, **E** = Strong

	SIZE	RATING
Cazadores	6 7/16" x 43	
Chavon	6½" x 41	**85**
Churchill	6¼" x 48	**82**
Club Seleccion Aristocrat	6¾" x 48	**83**
Club Seleccion Barons	8½" x 52	
Club Seleccion Nobles	6¼" x 44	
Club Seleccion Regals	7" x 50	**83**
Cortos	4" x 28	
Lonsdale	6½" x 42	**82**
Lonsdale Maduro	6½" x 42	
#1	6 13/16" x 42	**86**
#2	6¼" x 42	**88**
#3	6 13/16" x 36	
#4	5½" x 42	**87**
#4 Maduro	5½" x 42	**85**
#100	4½" x 50	**83**
#100 Maduro	4½" x 50	**86**
Panatela	5⅜" x 34	
Panatela Extra	6" x 34	
Presidente	6¾" x 44	**85**
Presidente Maduro	6¾" x 44	
Reales	6⅛" x 36	
Royal Corona	6" x 46	**81**
Soberano	7½" x 50	**89**
Soberano Maduro	7½" x 50	**87**

Private Stock Cigars

Dominican Republic **B**

Tabacos Dominicanos S.A.

	SIZE	RATING
No. 1	7¾" x 48	
No. 2	6" x 48	
No. 3	6½" x 33	
No. 4	5¾" x 38	
No. 5	5¾" x 43	
No. 6	5¼" x 46	
No. 7	4¾" x 43	
No. 8	4⅜" x 35	
No. 9	4⅝" x 26	
No. 10	4" x 40	
No. 11	4⅝" x 50	

Punch

Cuba **E**

	SIZE	RATING
Black Prince	5⅝" x 46	
Churchill	7" x 47	**91**
Corona	5½" x 42	**89**
Diademas Extra	9" x 47	**92**
Double Corona	7⅝" x 49	**91**
Gran Coronas	5¾" x 40	
Margaritas	4¾" x 26	
Monarcas	7" x 47	
Nacionales	5¼" x 42	
Ninfas	7" x 38	**88**
Panatelas	4⅔" x 34	
Panatelas Grandes	7" x 33	
Petit Coronas del Punch	5" x 42	
Petit Punch	4" x 40	
Petit Punch Deluxe	4" x 40	
Presidentes	5" x 42	
Punch	5½" x 46	**87**
Punch Punch	5⅝" x 46	
Royal Coronations	5⅔" x 42	
Royal Selection No. 12	5½" x 42	**86**
Souvenirs Deluxe	4⅞" x 40	
Très Petit Coronas	4⅓" x 42	

Punch

Honduras **C**

Villazon & Co.

	SIZE	RATING
After Dinner	7½" x 45	**74**
Amatista	6½" x 43	**84**
Britannia	6¼" x 50	
Cafe Royal	6" x 43	**88**
Casa Grande	7¼" x 46	
Chateau L	7⅜" x 52	**85**
Chateau L Maduro	7¼" x 54	**85**
Chateau M	5¾" x 46	**85**
Chateau M Maduro	6¾" x 46	**86**
Corona	6¼" x 45	**88**
Deluxe Series Chateau L	7½" x 52	**85**
Deluxe Series Chateau L Maduro	7¼" x 52	**85**
Deluxe Series Chateau M	5½" x 46	**85**
Deluxe Series Chateau M Maduro	5½" x 46	**86**
Deluxe Series Coronas	5¼" x 44	
Deluxe Series Royal Coronation	5¼" x 44	**83**
Diademas	7¼" x 54	
Double Corona	6¾" x 48	**85**
Double Corona Maduro	6¾" x 48	**86**
Elite	5¼" x 44	**85**
Gran Cru Britannia	6¼" x 50	**88**
Gran Cru Diademas	7¼" x 54	**82**
Gran Cru Monarch	6¾" x 48	**87**
Gran Cru Prince Consort	8½" x 52	**85**
Gran Cru Robusto	5¼" x 50	**84**
Gran Cru Superior	5½" x 48	
Gran Cru Superior Deluxe	5½" x 48	**83**
Largo Elegante	7" x 32	
London Club	5" x 40	
Lonsdale	6½" x 43	**85**
Monarcas	6¾" x 48	
#1	6⅝" x 43	**86**
#75	5½" x 43	**84**
Pita Maduro	6⅛" x 50	**87**
Presidente	8½" x 52	
Prince Consorts	8½" x 52	
Punch	6¼" x 45	**81**
Robustos	5¼" x 50	

	SIZE	RATING
Rothschild	4½" x 50	**84**
Rothschild Maduro	4½" x 50	**86**
Royal Coronation	5½" x 44	**83**
Slim Panatelas	4" x 28	
Super Rothschild	5½" x 50	**88**
Superiors	5½" x 48	

PUROS INDIOS
***Honduras* D**
Puros Indios Cigars, Inc.

	SIZE	RATING
Churchill Especial Colorado	7¼" x 53	
Churchill Especial Colorado Claro	7¼" x 53	
Churchill Especial Maduro	7¼" x 53	
Churchill Maduro	7¼" x 52	**86**
Corona Gorda	6" x 52	**86**
Corona Gorda Maduro	6" x 52	**86**
Nacionales Colorado	6½" x 43	
Nacionales Colorado Claro	6½" x 43	
Nacionales Maduro	6½" x 43	
No. 1 Especial Colorado	7" x 48	
No. 1 Especial Colorado Claro	7" x 48	
No. 1 Especial Maduro	7" x 48	
No. 2 Especial Colorado	6½" x 46	
No. 2 Especial Colorado Claro	6½" x 46	
No. 2 Especial Maduro	6½" x 46	
No. 4 Especial	5½" x 44	**90**
No. 4 Especial Colorado	5½" x 44	
No. 4 Especial Colorado Claro	5½" x 44	
No. 4 Especial Maduro	5½" x 44	
No. 5 Especial Colorado	5" x 36	**87**
No. 5 Especial Colorado Claro	5" x 36	**83**
Palmas Real Colorado	7" x 38	
Palmas Real Colorado Claro	7" x 38	
Palmas Real Maduro	7" x 38	
Petit Perla	5" x 38	**82**
Petit Perla Colorado Claro	5" x 38	
Petit Perla Maduro	5" x 38	
Presidente Colorado	7¼" x 47	
Presidente Colorado Claro	7¼" x 47	
Presidente Maduro	7¼" x 47	
Pyramid No. 1	7½" x 60	**92**
Pyramid No. 1 Colorado	7½" x 60	
Pyramid No. 1 Colorado Claro	7½" x 60	
Pyramid No. 1 Maduro	7½" x 60	
Pyramid No. 2	6½" x 46	**90**
Pyramid No. 2 Colorado Claro	6½" x 46	
Pyramid No. 2 Maduro	6½" x 46	
Rothschild Colorado	5" x 50	**87**
Rothschild Colorado Claro	5" x 50	
Rothschild Maduro	5" x 50	
Toro Especial Colorado	6" x 50	
Toro Especial Colorado Claro	6" x 50	

QUAI D'ORSAY
***Cuba* C**

	SIZE	RATING
Corona Claro	5½" x 42	
Corona Claro Claro	5½" x 42	
Gran Corona	6⅛" x 42	
Imperiales	7" x 47	**90**
Panatela	7" x 33	

QUINTERO
***Cuba* C**

	SIZE	RATING
Churchill	6½" x 42	**92**
Coronas	5½" x 42	
Coronas Selectas	5½" x 42	
Medias Coronas	5" x 40	**84**

RAFAEL GONZALEZ
***Cuba* D**

	SIZE	RATING
Coronas Extra	5⅝" x 46	
Demi Tasse	4" x 30	
Lonsdale	6½" x 42	**91**
Panatelas	4⅔" x 34	
Petit Corona	5" x 42	
Petit Lonsdale	5" x 42	
Slenderellas	7" x 28	
Très Petit Corona	4⅓" x 40	
Très Petit Lonsdale	4½" x 40	

RAMON ALLONES
***Cuba* D**

	SIZE	RATING
Allones Specially Selected	4⅞" x 50	
Corona	5½" x 42	**89**
Gigantes	7⅝" x 49	**94**
8-9-8	6⅔" x 43	
Ideales	6½" x 40	**89**
No. 66 (perfecto)	6" x n/a	**87**
Petit Corona	5" x 42	
Ramonitas	4¾" x 26	
Small Club Corona	4⅓" x 42	
Specially Selected	5" x 50	**91**

Strength Key: A = Mild, **B** = Mild to Medium, **C** = Medium, **D** = Medium to Strong, **E** = Strong

Ramon Allones

Dominican Republic **B**

General Cigar Co.

	SIZE	RATING
"A"	7" x 45	**85**
"B"	6½" x 42	**87**
"D"	5" x 42	**86**
Crystal Tube	6½" x 43	**86**
Redondos	7" x 49	**85**
Trump	6¾" x 43	**83**

Rollers Choice

Dominican Republic **B**

Manufactura de Tabacos S.A. de C.V.

	SIZE	RATING
Cetros	5½" x 43	
Corona	6" x 43	
Double Corona	7" x 50	
Fino	5½" x 41	
Lonsdale	6½" x 46	
Pequeño	4¼" x 40	
Robusto	5" x 50	
Toros	6" x 50	
Torpedo	5½" x 56	

Romeo y Julieta

Cuba **D**

	SIZE	RATING
Alfred Dunhill Ltd. Selection No. 758	6½" x 42	**97**
Alfred Dunhill Ltd. Selection Sun-Grown	5½" x 44	**89**
Belicoso	5½" x 52	**90**
Belvedere	5½" x 39	**94**
Cazadores	6⅓" x 44	
Cedros De Luxe No. 1	6½" x 42	
Cedros De Luxe No. 2	5½" x 42	
Cedros De Luxe No. 3	5" x 42	
Celestiales Finos	5" x 46	**87**
Churchill	7" x 47	**92**
Club Kings	5" x 42	
Corona	5½" x 42	**89**
Coronas Grandes	6⅛" x 42	**90**
Excepcionales	5" x 42	
Exhibición No. 3	5½" x 46	**91**
Exhibición No. 4	5" x 48	**92**
Fabulosos	9" x 47	**91**
Julietas	4½" x 40	
Nacionales	5¼" x 42	
Palmas Reales	7" x 33	
Panatelas	4⅔" x 34	
Petit Corona	5" x 42	**89**
Petit Julietas	4" x 30	
Petit Princess	4" x 40	
Plateados de Romeo	5" x 40	
Prince of Wales	7" x 47	
Romeo No. 1 De Luxe	5½" x 42	
Romeo No. 2 De Luxe	5" x 42	
Romeo No. 3 De Luxe	4⅔" x 40	
Shakespeare	6½" x 28	**85**
Sun-Grown Brevas	5½" x 44	**89**
Très Petit Corona	4½" x 40	

Romeo y Julieta

Dominican Republic **B**

Manufactura de Tabacos S.A. de C.V.

	SIZE	RATING
Brevas	5⅝" x 38	
Cetro	6½" x 44	
Chiquitas	4¼" x 32	
Churchill	7" x 50	**83**
Corona	5½" x 44	**83**
Delgados	7" x 32	
Monarca	8" x 52	
Palma	6" x 43	**84**
Panatela	5¼" x 35	
Presidente	7" x 43	**88**
Romeo	6" x 46	**85**
Rothschild	5" x 50	**87**
Rothschild Maduro	5" x 50	**87**
Vintage I	6" x 42	**87**
Vintage II	6" x 46	**87**
Vintage III	4½" x 50	**86**
Vintage IV	7" x 48	**85**
Vintage V	7½" x 50	**89**
Vintage VI	6½" x 60	

Royal Dominicana

Dominican Republic **B**

Manufactura de Tabacos S.A. de C.V.

	SIZE	RATING
Churchill	7¼" x 50	
Corona	6" x 46	
Nacional	5½" x 43	
No. 1	6¾" x 43	
Super Fino	6" x 35	

Royal Jamaica

Jamaica **B**

Consolidated Cigar Corp.

	SIZE	RATING
Buccaneer	5½" x 30	**88**
Buccaneer Maduro	5½" x 30	
Churchill	8" x 51	
Churchill Maduro	8" x 51	**86**
Corona	5½" x 40	**87**
Corona Maduro	5½" x 40	**87**
Corona Grande	6½" x 42	**84**
Corona Grande Maduro	6½" x 42	**85**
Corona Maduro	5½" x 40	**87**
Director	6" x 45	**87**
Double Corona	7" x 45	**87**
Doubloon	7" x 30	
Gauchos	5" x 33	**85**
Giant Corona	7½" x 49	**83**
Goliath	9" x 64	**80**
Individuals	8½" x 52	
Navarro	6¾" x 34	

	SIZE	RATING
New York Plaza	6" x 40	
No. 1 Tube	6" x 45	82
No. 2 Tube	6½" x 34	85
No. 10 Downing Street	10" x 51	
Park Lane	6" x 47	85
Petit Corona	5" x 40	83
Pirate	4½" x 30	
Rapier	6½" x 28	
Robusto	4½" x 49	85
Royal Corona	6" x 40	

SAINT LUIS REY
Cuba   **D**

Churchill	7" x 47	89
Coronas	5½" x 42	
Lonsdale	6½" x 42	88
Regios	5" x 48	
Serie A	5⅝" x 46	

SAINT LUIS REY
Honduras   **C**
Tabacos Rancho Jamastran

Churchill	7" x 50	
Lonsdale	6½" x 44	86
Serie A	6" x 50	85
Torpedo	6" x 54	

SANCHO PANZA
Cuba   **D**

Bachilleres	4½" x 40	
Belicoso	5½" x 52	86
Coronas	5½" x 42	
Coronas Gigantes	7" x 47	
Dorados	6½" x 42	
Molinas	6½" x 42	91
Non Plus	5" x 42	85
Sanchos	9¼" x 47	86
Tronquitos	5½" x 42	

SANCHO PANZA
Honduras   **B**
Villazon & Co.

Cuban No. 4	5" x 42	
Habaneros	6¼" x 45	
Miramar	6" x 50	
Sanchos	9¼" x 47	86
Seville	7½" x 50	

SANTA CLARA
Mexico   **C**
Tabacos Santa Clara

I	7½" x 52	87
I Maduro	7½" x 52	
II	6½" x 48	78
II Maduro	6½" x 48	
III	6¾" x 43	85
III Maduro	6¾" x 43	

	SIZE	RATING
IV	5" x 44	
IV Maduro	5" x 44	
V	6" x 43	87
V Maduro	6" x 44	
VI	6" x 50	79
VII	5½" x 25	
VII Maduro	5½" x 25	
VIII	n/a x n/a	
No. 1830	6" x 50	85
Premier Tubes	6¾" x 38	
Quino	4¼" x 30	
Robusto	4½" x 50	72
Robusto Maduro	4½" x 50	

SANTA DAMIANA
Dominican Republic   **C**
Consolidated Cigar Corp.

#100	6¾" x 48	83
#300	5½" x 46	83
#500	5" x 50	84
#700	6½" x 42	82
#800	7" x 50	84

SANTA MARIA
Dominican Republic   **C**
Manufactura de Tabacos S.A. de C.V.

#1	7" x 50	
#2	6¾" x 38	
#3	5½" x 43	

SANTA ROSA
Honduras   **C**
Flor de La Copan

Cetros	6" x 42	86
Churchill	7" x 49	87
Corona	6½" x 44	83
Elegante	7" x 43	
Embajadores	7" x 43	
Largos	6¾" x 35	
Numero Cuatro	5½" x 42	86
Regulares	5½" x 45	
Sancho Panza Maduro	4½" x 50	81
Toro	6" x 50	86

SAVINELLI EXTREMELY LIMITED RESERVE
Dominican Republic   **C**
Tabacalera Arturo Fuente y Cia.

E.L.R. #1 Churchill	7¼" x 48	88
E.L.R. #2 Corona Extra	6⅝" x 46	
E.L.R. #3 Lonsdale	6¼" x 43	88
E.L.R. #4 Double Corona	6" x 50	87
E.L.R. #5 Extraordinaire	5½" x 44	89
E.L.R. #6 Robusto	5" x 49	88

Strength Key: A = Mild, **B** = Mild to Medium, **C** = Medium, **D** = Medium to Strong, **E** = Strong

SAVINELLI ORO
Dominican Republic C
La Aurora S.A.

	Size	Rating
ORO 750 #1 Churchill	7" x 47	
ORO 750 #2 Lonsdale	6½" x 44	
ORO 750 #3 Robusto	5" x 50	
ORO 750 #4 Corona Gorda	6⅜" x 48	
ORO 750 #5 Corona	5$\frac{9}{16}$" x 42	

SIGLO 21
Dominican Republic B
Puros de Villa Gonzalez S.A.

	Size	Rating
#1	4½" x 50	
#2	6½" x 44	
#3	6" x 50	
#4	7" x 48	
#5	8" x 50	
21-4	7" x 48	

SIGNATURE COLLECTION BY SANTIAGO CABANA
U.S.A. & Dominican Republic D
Caribbean Cigar Co.

	Size	Rating
Caribe	5½" x 44	
Chica	5" x 38	
Churchill	7¼" x 50	
Corona	6½" x 42	
Double Corona	7½" x 46	
Lancero	7½" x 38	
Presidente	7½" x 54	
Robusto	5" x 50	87
Torpedo	6½" x 54	90

SOSA
Dominican Republic C
Tabacalera A. Fuente y Cia.

	Size	Rating
Brevas	5½" x 43	84
Brevas Maduro	5½" x 43	
Churchill	7" x 48	88
Churchill Maduro	7" x 48	88
Family Selection Intermezzo	5" x 32	
Family Selection No. 1	6¾" x 43	85
Family Selection No. 2	6¼" x 54	88
Family Selection No. 3	5¾" x 44	
Family Selection No. 4	5" x 40	
Family Selection No. 5	5" x 50	86
Family Selection No. 6	6¼" x 38	82
Family Selection No. 7	6" x 50	
Family Selection No. 8	6¾" x 48	
Family Selection No. 9	7¾" x 52	
Governor	6" x 50	88
Governor Maduro	6" x 50	
Lonsdale	6½" x 43	78
Lonsdale Maduro	6½" x 43	
Magnums	7½" x 52	
Magnums Maduro	7½" x 52	
No. 1	6½" x 43	87
Pyramid #2	7" x 64	80
Pyramid #2 Maduro	7" x 64	
Rothschild Maduro	4¾" x 49	88
Santa Fe	6" x 35	85
Santa Fe Maduro	6" x 35	
Soberano	7½" x 52	88
Wavell	4¾" x 50	88
Wavell Maduro	4¾" x 50	87

TABACALERA
Philippines A/B
La Flor de la Isabella, Inc.

	Size	Rating
Banderilla	7¼" x 38	
Breva	5$\frac{5}{16}$" x 44	
Conde de Guell	6⅝" x 38	
Coronas	5½" x 42	
Coronas Largas	6½" x 44	
Coronas Largas Especiales	8" x 47	
Cortado	5⅛" x 45	
Double Corona	8½" x 50	
Gigantes	14¼" x 72	
Half Corona	4" x 37	
Panatelas	5" x 35	
Panatelas Larga	5¾" x 35	
Robusto	5" x 50	

TABAQUERO
Dominican Republic A
Palma Industries

	Size	Rating
542	5" x 42	82
638	6" x 38	
644	6" x 50	
650	6" x 50	
746	7" x 46	
754	7" x 54	
850	8" x 50	

TE-AMO
Mexico C
Nueva Matacan Tabacos S.A. de C.V.

	Size	Rating
C.E.O.	8½" x 52	82
C.E.O. Maduro	8½" x 52	
Caballero	7" x 35	
Celebration	6¾" x 44	81
Churchill	7½" x 50	82
Churchill Lite	7½" x 50	
Churchill Maduro	7½" x 50	84
Double Perfecto	7" x 52	
Double Perfecto Maduro	7" x 52	
Elegante	5½" x 30	
Elegante Light	5¾" x 27	
Epicure	5" x 30	
Figurado	6½" x 50	85
Figurado Maduro	6½" x 50	

	SIZE	RATING
Gran Piramide	7¼" x 54	**84**
Gran Piramide Maduro	7¼" x 54	
Impulse Lights	5" x 32	**81**
Intermezzo	4" x 28	
Maximo Churchill	7" x 54	
Maximo Churchill Maduro	7" x 54	**86**
Meditation	6" x 42	**85**
Meditation Light	6" x 42	
Meditation Maduro	6" x 42	
No. 4	5" x 42	**83**
Pauser	5⅜" x 35	
Picador	7" x 27	
Picador Maduro	7" x 27	
Piramide	6" x 50	**83**
Piramide Maduro	6" x 50	
Presidente	7" x 50	**84**
Presidente Maduro	7" x 50	**83**
Relaxation	6⅝" x 44	**82**
Relaxation Maduro	6⅝" x 44	
Robusto	5½" x 54	
Robusto Maduro	5½" x 54	**81**
Satisfaction Maduro	6" x 46	**82**
Torero	6½" x 35	**81**
Torero Light	6 9/16" x 35	
Torito	4¾" x 50	**82**
Torito Maduro	4¾" x 50	**85**
Toro	6" x 50	**86**
Toro Light	6" x 50	
Toro Maduro	6" x 50	**84**

TE-AMO NEW YORK, NEW YORK
Mexico C
Nueva Matacan Tabacos S.A. de C.V.

	SIZE	RATING
Broadway	7¼" x 48	
5th Avenue	5½" x 44	
La Guardia	5" x 54	**87**
Park Avenue	6⅝" x 42	**80**
7th Avenue	6½" x 46	
Wall Street	6" x 52	**84**

TEMPLE HALL
Jamaica C
General Cigar Co.

	SIZE	RATING
Belicoso	6" x 50	**88**
No. 450	4½" x 49	
No. 450 Maduro	4½" x 49	**86**
No. 500	5" x 31	
No. 550	5½" x 50	**86**
No. 625	6¼" x 42	**82**
No. 675	6¾" x 45	
No. 685	6⅞" x 34	**87**
No. 700	7½" x 49	**84**

TESOROS DE COPAN
Honduras C
Cigars of Honduras

	SIZE	RATING
Cetros	6¼" x 44	**84**
Churchill	7" x 50	
Corona	5¼" x 46	**77**
Lindas	5⅝" x 38	**85**
Toros	6" x 50	
Yumbo	4¾" x 50	

THE GRIFFIN'S
Dominican Republic C
Tabacos Dominicanos S.A.

	SIZE	RATING
Don Bernardo	9" x 46	**85**
Griffiños	3¾" x 18	
No. 100	7" x 38	**84**
No. 200	7" x 44	**81**
No. 300	6⅔" x 42	**84**
No. 400	6" x 38	**86**
No. 500	5 1/16" x 50	
Prestige	8" x 48	**85**
Privilege	5" x 30	**86**
Robusto	5" x 50	**88**

THOMAS HINDS HONDURAN SELECTION
Honduras C
Nestor Plasencia

	SIZE	RATING
Churchill	7" x 49	**88**
Corona	5½" x 42	**86**
Presidente	8½" x 52	**87**
Robusto	5" x 50	**84**
Royal Corona	6" x 43	
Short Churchill	6" x 50	**82**
Supremos	7" x 43	**85**
Torpedo	6" x 52	**86**

THOMAS HINDS NICARAGUAN SELECTION
Nicaragua C
Tabacos Puros de Nicaragua

	SIZE	RATING
Cabinet Selection Robusto	5" x 50	**87**
Churchill	7" x 49	
Churchill Maduro	7" x 49	**83**
Corona	5½" x 42	**84**
Corona Maduro	5½" x 42	
Corona Gorda	6" x 50	**84**
Corona Gorda Maduro	6" x 50	**84**
Lonsdale	6⅔" x 43	**87**
Lonsdale Extra	7" x 43	
Lonsdale Extra Maduro	7" x 43	
Robusto	5" x 50	**85**
Robusto Maduro	5" x 50	**84**
Short Churchill	6" x 50	**85**

Strength Key: A = Mild, **B** = Mild to Medium, **C** = Medium, **D** = Medium to Strong, **E** = Strong

	SIZE	RATING
Short Churchill Maduro	6" x 50	
Torpedo	6" x 52	
Torpedo Maduro	6" x 52	

TOPPER
Honduras **B**
Nestor Plasencia

Churchill	7½" x 50	
Corona	5½" x 43	
Numero Uno	6½" x 43	
Panatela	7" x 34	
Rothschild	4½" x 50	
Toro	6" x 50	

TOPPER CENTENNIAL
Dominican Republic **B**
Manufactura de Tabacos S.A. de C.V.

Lonsdale	6¾" x 43	
Toro	6" x 50	

TRESADO
Dominican Republic **A**
Consolidated Cigar Corp.

Selección #100	8" x 53	
Selección #200	7" x 48	83
Selección #200 Maduro	7" x 48	89
Selección #300	6" x 46	84
Selección #400	6⅝" x 44	86
Selección #500	5½" x 42	85
Selección #500 Maduro	5½" x 42	83

TROYA
Dominican Republic **C**
Tabacos Dominicanos S.A.

Clasica	5½" x 42	84
Clasica #27	5½" x 42	
Clasica #72	7½" x 50	
#18 Rothschild	4½" x 50	83
#18 Rothschild Maduro	4½" x 50	87
#27 Corona	5½" x 42	87
#36 Palma Fina	7" x 36	
#45 Cetro	6¼" x 44	90
#45 Cetro Maduro	6¼" x 44	83
#54 Elegante	7" x 43	86
#54 Elegante Maduro	7" x 43	
#63 Churchill	6⅞" x 46	86
#63 Churchill Maduro	6⅞" x 46	84
#72 Executive	7¾" x 50	82
#72 Executive Maduro	7¾" x 50	
#81 Torpedo	7" x 54	87
#81 Torpedo Maduro	7" x 54	

V CENTENNIAL
Honduras **C/D**
Nestor Plasencia

Cetro	6¼" x 44	89
Cetro Maduro	6¼" x 44	
Churchill	7" x 48	87
Churchill Maduro	6⅞" x 48	84
Corona	5½" x 42	83
Numero 1	7½" x 38	88
Numero 2	6" x 50	88
Numero 2 Maduro	6" x 50	84
Presidente	8" x 50	83
Robusto	5" x 50	87
Robusto Maduro	5" x 50	85
Torpedo	7" x 54	87

VARGAS
Canary Islands **C/D**
Tabacos Vargas SL

Capitolios	5⅛" x 44	
Churchill	7½" x 50	
Diplomaticos	5½" x 36	77
Presidentes	6¾" x 46	
Reserva Cenadores	5½" x 46	84
Robusto	4¾" x 50	83

VIRTUOSO
Honduras **C**
Nestor Plasencia

Cetros	6" x 43	
Double Corona	6" x 50	
Double Corona Maduro	6" x 50	
Lonsdale	7" x 44	
Lonsdale Maduro	7" x 44	
Presidente	8" x 52	
Presidente Maduro	8" x 52	
Robusto	4¾" x 52	
Robusto Maduro	4¾" x 52	

VUELTABAJO
Dominican Republic **C**
Cuervo y Hermano

Churchill	6¾" x 48	83
Corona	5½" x 42	86
Gigante	8½" x 52	83
Lonsdale	6½" x 43	80
Pyramid	7" x 54	84
Robusto	4½" x 50	86
Toro	6" x 50	82

	SIZE	RATING
ZINO		
Honduras C		
La Flor de Copan		
Diamonds	5½" x 40	**86**
Elegance	6¾" x 34	
Juniors	6½" x 30	**81**
Mouton–Cadet No. 1	6½" x 44	**86**
Mouton–Cadet No. 2	6" x 35	**83**
Mouton–Cadet No. 3	5¾" x 36	**85**
Mouton–Cadet No. 4	5⅛" x 30	**86**
Mouton–Cadet No. 5	5" x 42	**87**
Mouton–Cadet No. 6	5" x 50	**82**

	SIZE	RATING
Princesse	4¼" x 20	
Tradition	6¼" x 44	**84**
Tubos No. 1	6¾" x 34	
Veritas	7" x 50	**86**
ZINO CONNOISSEUR SERIES		
Honduras C		
La Flor de Copan		
100	7½" x 52	
200	6½" x 48	
300	5¾" x 46	

GLOSSARY

Many of the words defined below appear within this handbook. Other words, not found in this handbook, are defined here for later reference—they will likely come up in conversation with other aficionados.

Amarillo—Designates a yellow wrapper leaf grown under shade.

Amatista—A glass jar containing 50 cigars (occasionally 25), sealed to be sold "factory fresh."

Belicoso—Traditionally a short, pyramid-shaped cigar, 5 or 5½ inches in length with a shorter, more rounded taper at the head and a ring gauge generally of 50 or less. Today, "belicoso" is frequently used to describe coronas or corona gordas with a tapered head.

Binder—The portion of a tobacco leaf used to hold together the "bunch."

Blend—The mixture of different types of tobacco in a cigar, including up to four types of filler leaves. Blending is an art, and professional blenders are responsible for maintaining a brand's signature taste from year to year.

Bloom—A naturally occurring phenomenon in the cigar aging process, also called plume, caused by the oils which are exuded during later stages of fermentation. It appears as a fine, white powder that can be brushed off. Not to be confused with cigar mold, which is bluish in color and stains the wrapper.

Boîte Nature—The cedar box in which many cigars are sold.

Book Style—The lengthwise style in which most better cigar filler leaves are folded. This is best done by hand. Machine-made cigars tend to use chopped filler.

Bouquet—The smell, or "nose," of a fine cigar. Badly-stored cigars lose their bouquet.

Box—Cigar boxes come in all shapes and sizes. Traditional styles include:
• cabinet selection: wood boxes with a sliding top designed to hold 25 or

50 cigars. • 8-9-8: a round-sided box specifically designed to accommo-date three rows of cigars—eight on top, nine in the middle, and eight on the bottom. • flat top, or 13-topper: a flat, rectangular box with 13 cigars on top and 12 on the bottom, divided by a spacer.

Box-pressed—The slightly squarish appearance taken on by cigars packed tightly in a box.

Bulk—A large pile of tobacco leaves in which fermentation occurs.

Bull's-Eye Piercer—A device for opening the closed head of a cigar before smoking. It creates a circular opening like a target's bull's eye.

Bunch—The mass of up to four different types of filler tobacco that are blended and held together by the binder to form the body of a cigar.

Bundle—A packaging method, designed with economy in mind, that uses a cellophane overwrap. It usually contains 25 or 50 cigars, traditionally without bands. Seconds from premium brands are often sold in bundles.

Burros—The piles, or bulks, in which cigar tobacco is fermented. They can be as tall as a person and are carefully monitored. If the heat level inside them gets too high (over 110°F), the burro is taken apart to slow the fermentation.

Cabinet selection—Cigars packed in a wooden box rather than the standard cardboard or paper covered cigar boxes. These are preferable when buying cigars for aging.

Candela—A bright green shade of wrapper, achieved by a heat-curing process that fixes the chlorophyll content of wrapper leaves prior to fer-mentation. Also referred to as "double claro."

Cap—A circular piece of wrapper leaf place at the head of a cigar to secure the wrapper. A good cut will leave part of the cap intact.

Capa—The cigar's wrapper.

Carotene—A naturally-occuring compound found in aged cigars.

Case—In the cigar production process, workers "case," or slightly moist-en, aged tobacco so that it will be easy for hand rollers to work with.

Cedar—The kind of wood that is used to make most cigar boxes and humidors.

Chaveta—A knife used by rollers in cigar factories to cut wrapper leaves.

Churchill—1. A large corona-format cigar, often 7 inches by a 48 ring gauge. 2. Sir Winston Churchill, who was famous for almost never being seen without a cigar.

Cigar Band—A ring of paper wrapped around the closed head of most cigars. Legend says that cigar bands were invented by Catherine the Great or by Spanish nobles to keep their gloves from being stained. Others credit this invention to a Dutch advertising and promotion genius named Gustave Bock, who stated that the band helped keep the cigar wrapper together. Cigar bands are often printed with the name of the brand, country of origin, and/or indication that the cigar is hand-rolled. They also often have colorful graphics which have made them popular collectors' items. In many folk tales, a cigar band served as a wedding band in impromptu ceremonies. For the record, it is equally appropriate to leave the band on while smoking a cigar or to remove it, as long as the cigar's wrapper leaf is not torn when the band is removed.

Cigarillos—Favored by some aficionados and scorned by others, these thin, three-inch cigars, popular in Europe, are generally machine-made, and many brands use homogenized wrappers or binders.

Claro—A pale-green to light-brown shade of wrapper, characteristic of wrapper leaves grown in the shade.

Colorado—A medium-brown to brownish-red shade of wrapper leaf.

Connecticut Broadleaf—A dark wrapper leaf often used for maduro cigars; grown in the United States in the Connecticut River Valley.

Connecticut Shade—A smooth, elastic, brown wrapper leaf used for premium cigars; grown in the United States in the Connecticut River Valley. As the name implies, it is grown under cheesecloth tents called *tapados*.

Corojos—Plants which are chosen to provide wrapper leaves and are grown under a gauze sunscreen.

Corona—The most familiar size and shape for premium cigars: generally straight-sided with an open foot and a closed, rounded head.

Cuban Seed—Usually refers to plants grown in non-Cuban countries with seeds from Cuba.

Cubatabaco—The worldwide distribution company for Cuban cigars— now called Habanos SA.

Culebra—A cigar made up of three panatelas braided and banded together; usually 5 to 6 inches in length, most often with a 38 ring gauge.

Diademas—A big cigar with a closed and tapered head. Generally about 8 inches long; the foot may be open, or closed like a perfecto.

Double Claro—(see Candela).

Double Corona, also called "prominente"—A big cigar, generally 7½ to 8 inches by a 49 to 52 ring gauge.

Draw—The amount of air that a smoker pulls through a lit cigar. A well-made cigar draws easily, yielding cool smoke. If the draw is too easy, the smoke will be too hot; if the cigar is plugged and the draw is tight, smoking it will not be relaxing.

Escaparates—Cooling cabinets in which cigars are kept at the factory for a few weeks after they have been rolled.

Fermentation—Like fine wines, fine cigar tobaccos are the product of fermentation and continue to go through additional stages of fermentation as they age. After the harvest, workers pile tobacco leaves into large "bulks," and moisten them to promote the primary fermentation. Temperatures inside a bulk may reach 140°F.

Figurado—A Spanish term that refers to cigars with exotic shapes, such as torpedos, pyramids, perfectos and culebras.

Filler Leaves—The individual tobacco leaves used in the body of the cigar. A fine cigar usually contains between two and four different types of filler tobacco.

Flag Leaves—An extension of the wrapper leaf shaped to finish the head of a cigar; used instead of a cap. Flags are sometimes tied off in a pigtail or a curly head.

Foot—The end of the cigar you light. In most types of cigars, it is pre-cut, but in torpedos and perfectos, it is sealed.

Gran Corona—A very big cigar; generally 9¼ inches by 47 ring gauge.

Gum—A tasteless vegetable adhesive used to secure the wrapper leaf.

Habano—A designation which, when inscribed on a cigar band, indicated that a cigar is Cuban. (Note: not all Cuban cigars are marked with "Habano" or "Havana.")

Habanos SA—the worldwide distribution company for Cuban cigars—formerly called Cubatabaco.

Half-wheel (media ruedas)—A bundle of 50 cigars. Cigar rollers usually use ribbon to tie the cigars they produce onto half-wheels.

Hand—A sheaf of harvested tobacco leaves tied together at the top. Hands are piled together to make a bulk for fermentation.

Hand-made—A cigar made entirely by hand with high-quality wrapper and long filler. All fine cigars are hand-made. Hand-rollers can generally use more delicate wrapper leaves than machines.

Hand-rolled—All hand-made cigars are hand-rolled, but some "hand-rolled" cigars are machine made up to the point when the wrapper is applied by hand.

Havana—1. The capital of Cuba, and the traditional center for manufacturing of Cuban cigars for export. 2. Cuban cigars are often called "Havanas," (or "Habanas"). 3. "Havana" is also used as a term to describe tobacco types grown from Cuban seed in places such as the Dominican Republic, Honduras, and Nicaragua.

Head—The closed end of the cigar; the end you cut before smoking.

Holder—Cigar holders are an interesting affectation and collectable, but true aficionados let nothing come between their lips and the head of a cigar they're smoking.

Homogenized Binder—Binder made of chopped tobacco leaf and cellulose. Scorned by purists, it facilitates machine production and can facilitate the burn of certain products.

Hot—a term used to describe a cigar that is underfilled and has a quick, loose draw. A hot cigar is likely to taste harsh, instead of mellow.

Humidor—A room or box designed to maintain the proper humidity and temperature for cigar preservation and aging. Humidity should remain around 70-percent, and temperature should stay in the 65°F to 70°F range.

Hygrometer—A device which indicates the humidity, or percentage of moisture in the air; used to monitor humidor conditions.

Inhale—What you don't do with cigar smoke.

Lance—A cutter used to pierce a small hole in the closed end of a cigar. Also called a piercer.

Lector—Traditionally, the person who reads to the cigar rollers while they do their work.

Ligero—An aromatic tobacco which is one of the three basic types of filler tobacco. The name means "light" in Spanish.

Long Filler—A term used to designate filler tobacco that runs the length of fine cigars. Machine-made cigars often use chopped filler.

Lonsdale—A long cigar format; generally 6¾ inches by a 42 to 44 ring gauge, but there are many variations.

Machine-made—Cigars made by machine use heavier-weight wrappers and binders and, in many cases, chopped filler instead of long filler.

Maduro—A shade of wrapper varying from a very dark reddish-brown to almost black. The color results from longer exposure to the sun, a cooking process, or longer fermentation. The word means "ripe" in Spanish.

Media Ruedas—See "Half-wheels."

Mini Cigarillo—another term for cigarillo.

Mold—1. A form used to shape the finished bunch for a cigar. It comes in two parts which are assembled and placed in a press. 2. A potentially damaging fungus that can form on cigars stored at too high a temperature.

Nicotine—Cigar tobacco loses much of its nicotine during the fermentation process. In addition, because cigar smoke is not inhaled, only the very limited moist surfaces in the mouth area absorb nicotine.

Oil—Oil is the mark of a well-humidified cigar. Even well-aged cigars secrete oil at 70 to 72 percent humidity, the level at which they should be stored.

Oscuro—A black shade of wrapper, darker than maduro, most often Brazilian or Mexican in origin.

Panatela—A long, thin cigar shape.

Parejos—Straight-sided cigars, such as coronas, panatelas and lonsdales.

Partidos—A prime tobacco growing area in Cuba.

Perfecto—A distinctive cigar shape that is closed at both ends, with a rounded head and a closed foot; usually with a bulge in the middle.

Period of Sickness—A time when cigars should not be smoked. Fresh cigars are fine, as are aged ones; but avoid cigars between three months and a year old.

Piercer—A cutter used to pierce a small hole in the closed end of a cigar. Also called a lance.

Planchas—Boards; tobacco leaves are spread on "planchas" before fermentation.

Plug—A blockage that sometimes occurs in the tobacco that can prevent a cigar from drawing properly. A plug can sometimes be alleviated by gently massaging the cigar.

Plugged—A description of a cigar that has a poor draw.

Purito—A small cigar, or cigarillo that more often than not is handmade, rather than machine made.

Pyramid—A sharply tapered cigar with a wide, open foot and a closed head.

Ring Gauge—A measurement of the diameter of a cigar, based on 64ths of an inch. A 40 ring gauge cigar is $^{40}/_{64}$ths of an inch thick.

Robusto—A substantial, but short cigar format; traditionally 5 to 5½ inches by a 50 ring gauge.

Seco—A type of filler tobacco which often contributes aroma and is usually medium-bodied. The word means "dry" in Spanish.

Shade-grown—Wrapper leaves that have been grown under a cheese cloth tent, called a tapado. The filtered sunlight creates a thinner, more elastic leaf.

Shoulder—The area of a cigar where the cap meets the body. If you cut into the shoulder the cigar will begin to unravel.

Spill—A strip of cedar used to light a cigar when using a candle or a fluid lighter, both of which can alter the taste of the cigar.

Sugar—Sugars occur naturally in tobacco. Darker wrappers, such as maduros, contain more sugar, making them sweeter.

Sun-grown—Tobacco grown in direct sunlight, which creates a thicker leaf with thicker veins.

Tapado—A cheese cloth tent under which "shade-grown" wrapper leaf is cultivated.

Tar—Because of the fermentation process, cigars have less tar than cigarettes.

Tercios—The large, palm bark-wrapped bales in which fermented tobacco is shipped to cigar factories.

Tooth—The grain pattern characteristic of less smooth wrapper leaf, such as leaf from Cameroon.

Torcedores—The experts who roll cigars in factories.

Torpedo—A cigar shape that features a closed foot, a pointed head, and a bulge in the middle.

Totalamente a Mano—Made totally by hand; a description found on cigar boxes. Much better than "Hecho a Mano," (made by hand, which can mean it is filled with machine-bunched filler), or "Envuelto a Mano," (packed by hand).

Tubos—Cigars packed in individual wood, metal or glass tubes to keep them fresh.

Tunneling—The unwelcome phenomenon of having your cigar burn unevenly. To prevent it, rotate your cigar now and then.

Vega—A tobacco plantation.

Vein—A structural part of a leaf; prominent veins can be a defect in wrappers.

Vintage—When a vintage is used for a cigar, it refers to the year the tobacco was harvested, not the year the cigar was made.

Viso—Designates a glossy wrapper leaf grown under cover.

Vuelta Abajo—The valley in Cuba that many believe produces the best cigar tobacco in the world.

Volado—A type of filler tobacco, added for its burning qualities.

Wedge Cut—A V-shaped cut made in the closed end of a cigar.

Wrapper—A high-quality tobacco leaf wrapped around a finished bunch and binder. It is very elastic and, at its best, unblemished.

INDEX

aftertaste, 25
agave, blue, 143
American Cancer Society, 23
Armagnac, 136
ash, 30
Bahia Province, 112
Belicoso, 128
binder leaf, 119
blue mold, 113
Blumenthal, Danny, 21, 62
Bons Bois, 135
Borderies, 135
Boruchin, Oscar, 21, 46, 66
Bourbon, 144
Brandy, 133, 137
Brazil, 112
Cameroon, 114
Candela, 123
Castro, Fidel, 149
cedar, 102
Central African Republic, 114
Champagne, 135
Churchill, 126
Cibao River, 112
Cigar Aficionado, 14, 151
cigar bands, 92
cigar dinners, 152
cigar smoke: and clothes, 92;
    exhaling, 93; tastes of, 25
cigar smoking: benefits of, 26;
    when to, 95; where to, 28;
    where not to, 91
cigarettes, 148, 150
cigars,
    aging, 121;
    appearance, 37;
    burn, 38;
    carrying, 105;
    at celebrations, 95;
    colors of, 123;

and Cognac, 133–136;
counterfeit, 111;
cutting, 83-86;
defective, 88;
draw, 38, 85;
evaluating, 37;
extinguishing, 27;
feel, 37;
flavor, 37;
health risks, 23;
how to hold, 27;
lighting, 87, 93;
re-lighting, 87;
restoration of, 104;
shapes of, 126;
sharing, 92;
sizes of, 126;
as a solace, 95,
and spirits, 133;
storing, 97;
straight sided, 126;
unusually shaped, 127;
varieties of, 38,
and women, 153
Claro, 123
Cognac, 133–136
Columbus, Christopher, 109
Connecticut Shade, 113
Connecticut Broadleaf, 113
Corona, 126
Craig, Elijah, 144
Cruz des Olmos, 112
Cuba, 109–110; U.S. trade
    embargo, 149
Cuban Revolution, 149
Culebra, 128
Cullman, Edgar M., 20, 67
cutters, 84, 93
Davidoff, Zino, 14, 20, 149
Diademas, 128

Dominican Republic, 111
Douro Valley, 138
Dunhill, Alfred, 14, 148
Ecuador, 112
etiquette, 91
Figurados, 127
finger-memory, 27
Fins Bois, 135
Fox, J.J., 14
Fuente, Carlos (Sr. and Jr.), 42, 58
Hollywood, 152
Honduras, 113
humidor, 97–99,
    choosing, 100;
    humidification devices, 101;
    maintenance of, 99;
    marrying of flavors within, 97;
    portable: 97, 105;
    walk-in, 36
Indonesia, 115
Java, 115
Kennedy, John F., 149, 164
lance, 85
Lewis, Robert, 14
Lonsdale, 127
Maduro, 113, 124;
    Mexican leaf, 113
Mexico, 113
moisture, 98
Natural, 124
Negro, 125
Nicaragua, 113
nicotine, 25, 85, 118
Oporto, 138
Oriente, 111
Oscuro, 125
Panatela, 127
Parejos, 126
Partido, 111
Perfecto, 128
Philippines, 115
piercer, 85
Pinar del Rio, 110
Port, 138

pyramid, 127
quintas, 138
Remedios, 111
ring gauge, 119
Robusto, 127
Rothman, Lew, 14, 21
Rothschild, Baroness
    Philippine de, 20
Rum, 142
San Andres Valley, 113
Sauter, Desmond, 14
scissors, 85
Semivuelta, 110
Sumatra, 115
tar, 85
taste, 25
Tequila, 174
Terry Report, 150
tobacco,
    aging, 118
    blends of, 119
    Cuban, 110
    Ecuadorian, 112
    fermentation: 117–118; in
        maduro wrappers, 124–125
    genetic makeup, 25
    growing, 117
    how raised/aged, 25
    Indonesian, 115
    sweating, 117
    United States, 113
tobacconist, 34–35
tooth, 115
torcedor, 119
Torpedo, 128
tubes, 106
Tubos, 106
Vuelta Abajo, 110
Whiskey: American, 144;
    Irish, 140
Whisky, Scotch, 141
women, and cigars, 93
wrapper leaf, 119, 123

PHOTOGRAPHY CREDITS

Cover design by Ken Newbaker
Cover photography by Jeff Harris

p. 6: Jeff Harris
p. 8: Courtney Grant Winston
pp. 11, 12: Kent Hanson
p. 13: Sara Matthews
p. 15: Dan Wagner
p. 17: James Suckling
p. 21: Dan Wagner
pp. 24, 26, 28: Sara Matthews
p. 29: AP/Wide World
    Photos, Inc.
p. 30: Jeff Harris
p. 32: Gentl & Hyers
p. 34: Rick Friedman/Blackstar
p. 35: Courtesy of Alfred Dunhill
    Ltd.
p. 36: Jon Wyand
p. 38: Arnold Zann/Blackstar
p: 40: Kent Hanson
pp. 42–81: Jeff Harris
pp. 82, 85: Gene Coleman
pp. 86, 88: Jeff Harris
p. 90: Sara Matthews
pp. 92, 94: G & J Images
p. 96: Kent Hanson (humidor
    from Elie Bleu)
p. 98: Gene Coleman
p. 99: James Worrell
p. 101: Sara Matthews
p. 102: Roger Jacobs
p. 103: Courtesy of Savinelli
p. 105: Marina Faust
p. 106: Jeff Harris

p. 108: James Suckling
p. 109: Wayne Eastep
p. 110: Courtesy of Richard B.
    Arkway, Inc.
p. 116: James Suckling
p. 118: Wayne Eastep
p. 119: Kent Hanson
pp. 120–121: James Suckling
p. 122: Kent Hanson
pp. 124–125, 129–132, 134:
    Jeff Harris
p. 136: Jonathan L. Smith
pp. 139, 141: Jeff Harris
p. 144: Sara Matthews
p. 146: Paul Rogers
p. 148: AP/Wide World
    Photos, Inc.
p. 149: Culver Pictures, Inc.
p. 150: UPI/Corbis-Bettmann
p. 153: Top, M. Gerber/LGI
    Photo Agency; Bottom,
    John Harding
pp. 154–155: James Suckling
    (Fidel Castro); Brad Trent
    (Wayne Gretsky); Stephen
    Wayda (Danny DeVito, Linda
    Evangelista, Demi Moore,
    Jack Nicholson, Arnold
    Schwarzenegger, Tom
    Selleck, James Woods);
    Courtney Grant Winston
    (Bill Cosby)
p. 157: The Kobal Collection
p. 159: Corbis-Bettmann
pp. 160, 162: Culver Pictures, Inc.